ROBERT SOUTHEY

by

EDWARD DOWDEN, M.A., Litt.D.

AUTHOR OF
" SHAKSPERE: A STUDY OF HIS MIND AND ART "
" SHAKSPERE PRIMER " ETC.

University Press of the Pacific
Honolulu, Hawaii

Robert Southey

by
Edward Dowden

ISBN: 1-4102-0874-5

NOTE.

I AM indebted throughout to *The Life and Correspondence of Robert Southey*, edited by the Rev. C. C. Southey, six volumes, 1850, and to *Selections from the Letters of Robert Southey*, edited by J. W. Warter, B.D., four volumes, 1856. Many other sources have been consulted. I thank Mr. W. J. Craig for help given in examining Southey manuscripts, and Mr. T. W. Lyster for many valuable suggestions.

CONTENTS.

SOUTHEY.

CHAPTER I.

CHILDHOOD.

No one of his generation lived so completely in and for literature as did Southey. "He is," said Byron, "the only existing entire man of letters." With him literature served the needs both of the material life and of the life of the intellect and imagination; it was his means of earning daily bread, and also the means of satisfying his highest ambitions and desires. This, which was true of Southey at five-and-twenty years of age, was equally true at forty, fifty, sixty. During all that time he was actively at work accumulating, arranging, and distributing knowledge; no one among his contemporaries gathered so large a store from the records of the past; no one toiled with such steadfast devotion to enrich his age; no one occupied so honourable a place in so many provinces of literature. There is not, perhaps, any single work of Southey's the loss of which would be felt by us as a capital misfortune. But the more we consider his total work, its mass, its variety, its high excellence, the more we come to regard it as a memorable, an extraordinary achievement.

1*

Southey himself, however, stands above his works. In subject they are disconnected, and some of them appear like huge fragments. It is the presence of one mind, one character in all, easily recognizable by him who knows Southey, which gives them a vital unity. We could lose the *History of Brazil*, or the *Peninsular War*, or the *Life of Wesley*, and feel that if our possessions were diminished, we ourselves in our inmost being had undergone no loss which might not easily be endured. But he who has once come to know Southey's voice as the voice of a friend, so clear, so brave, so honest, so full of boyish glee, so full of manly tenderness, feels that if he heard that voice no more a portion of his life were gone. To make acquaintance with the man is better than to study the subjects of his books. In such a memoir as the present, to glance over the contents of a hundred volumes, dealing with matters widely remote, would be to wander upon a vast circumference when we ought to strike for the centre. If the reader come to know Southey as he read and wrote in his library, as he rejoiced and sorrowed among his children, as he held hands with good old friends, as he walked by the lake-side, or lingered to muse near some mountain stream, as he hoped and feared for England, as he thought of life and death and a future beyond the grave, the end of this small book will have been attained.

At the age of forty-six Robert Southey wrote the first of a series of autobiographic sketches; his spirit was courageous, and life had been good to him; but it needed more than his courage to live again in remembrance with so many of the dead; having told the story of his boyhood, he had not the heart to go farther. The autobiography rambles pleasantly into by-ways of old Bath and Bristol life; at Westminster School it leaves him. So far

we shall go along with it; for what lies beyond, a record
of Southey's career must be brought together from a mul-
titude of letters, published or still remaining in manuscript,
and from many and massy volumes in prose and verse,
which show how the industrious hours sped by.

Southey's father was a linen-draper of Bristol. He had
left his native fields under the Quantock hills to take service in a London shop, but his heart suffered in its exile.
The tears were in his eyes one day when a porter went by
carrying a hare, and the remembrance suddenly came to
him of his rural sports. On his master's death he took a
place behind the counter of Britton's shop in Wine Street,
Bristol; and when, twelve years later, he opened a shop for
himself in the same business, he had, with tender reminis-
cence, a hare painted for a device upon his windows. He
kept his grandfather's sword which had been borne in
Monmouth's rebellion; he loved the chimes and quarter-
boys of Christ Church, Bristol, and tried, as church-warden,
to preserve them. What else of poetry there may have
been in the life of Robert Southey the elder is lost among
the buried epics of prosaic lives. We cannot suppose that
as a man of business he was sharp and shrewd; he certainly was not successful. When the draper's work was
done, he whiled away the hours over Felix Farley's Bristol
Journal, his only reading. For library some score of books
shared with his wine-glasses the small cupboard in the
back parlour; its chief treasures were the *Spectator*, the
Guardian, some eighteenth-century poems, dead even then,
and one or two immortal plays.

On Sundays Mr. Southey, then a bachelor, would stroll
to Bedminster to dine at the pleasant house of Mrs. Hill
—a substantial house to which Edward Hill, gentleman,
brought his second wife, herself a widow; a house rich in

old English comfort, with its diamond-tiled garden-way and jessamine-covered porch, its wainscoted "best kitchen," its blue room and green room and yellow room, its grapes and greengages and nectarines, its sweet-williams and stocks and syringas. Among these pleasant surroundings the young draper found it natural, on Sabbath afternoons, to make love to pleasant Margaret Hill. "Never," writes her son Robert Southey—"never was any human being blessed with a sweeter temper or a happier disposition." Her face had been marred by the seams of small-pox, but its brightness and kindness remained; there was a charm in her clear hazel eyes, so good a temper and so alert an understanding were to be read in them. She had not gone to any school except one for dancing, and "her state," declares Southey, "was the more gracious;" her father had, however, given her lessons in the art of whistling; she could turn a tune like a blackbird. From a mother, able to see a fact swiftly and surely, and who knew both to whistle and to dance, Southey inherited that alertness of intellect and that joyous temper, without which he could not have accomplished his huge task-work, never yielding to a mood of rebellion or *ennui*.

After the courtship on Sunday afternoons came the wedding, and before long a beautiful boy was born, who died in infancy. On the 12th of August, 1774, Mrs. Southey was again in the pain of childbirth. "Is it a boy?" she asked the nurse. "Ay, a great ugly boy!" With such salutation from his earliest critic the future poet-laureate entered this world. "God forgive me," his mother exclaimed afterwards, in relating the event, "when I saw what a great red creature it was, covered with rolls of fat, I thought I should never be able to love him." In due time the red creature proved to be a distinctively human child, whose curly hair and sensitive feelings made him a mother's darling. He had not yet heard of sentiment or of Rousseau, but he wept at the pathos of romantic literature, at the tragic fate of the " Children sliding on the ice all on a summer's day," or the too early death of " Billy Pringle's pig," and he would beg the reciters not to proceed. His mother's household cares multiplied, and Southey, an unbreeched boy of three years, was borne away one morning by his faithful foster-mother Patty to be handed over to the tender mercies of a schoolmistress. Ma'am Powell was old and grim, and with her lashless eyes gorgonized the new pupil; on the seizure of her hand he woke to rebellion, kicking lustily, and crying, " Take me to Pat! I don't like ye! you've got ugly eyes! take me to Pat, I say !" But soft-hearted Pat had gone home, sobbing.

Mrs. Southey's one weakness was that of submitting too meekly to the tyranny of an imperious half-sister, Miss Tyler, the daughter of Grandmother Hill by her first marriage. For this weakness there were excuses; Miss Tyler was an elder sister by many years; she had property of her own; she passed for a person of fashion, and was still held to be a beauty; above all, she had the advantage of a temper so capricious and violent that to quarrel with her at all might be to lose her sisterly regard for ever. Her struggling sister's eldest son took Aunt Tyler's fancy; it was a part of her imperious kindness to adopt or half-adopt the boy. Aunt Tyler lived in Bath; in no other city could a gentlewoman better preserve health and good looks, or enjoy so much society of distinction on easy but not too ample means; it possessed a charming theatre, and Miss Tyler was a patron of the drama. To Bath, then, she had brought her portrait by Gainsborough, her inlaid cabinet of ebony, her cherry-wood arm-chair, her mezzotints after Angelica Kaufmann, her old-maid hoards of this and of that, the woman servant she had saved from the toils of matrimony, and the old man, harmless as one of the crickets which he nightly fed until he died. To Bath Miss Tyler also brought her nephew; and she purchased a copy of the new gospel of education, Rousseau's *Emilius*, in order to ascertain how Nature should have her perfect work with a boy in petticoats. Here the little victim, without companions, without play, without the child's beatitudes of dirt and din, was carefully swathed in the odds and ends of habits and humours which belonged to a maiden lady of a whimsical, irrational, and self-indulgent temper. Miss Tyler, when not prepared for company, wandered about the house—a faded beauty—in the most faded and fluttering of costumes; but in her rags she was spotless. To preserve herself and her worldly gear from the dust, for ever floating and gathering in this our sordid atmosphere, was the business of her life. Her acquaintances she divided into the clean and the unclean—the latter class being much the more numerous. Did one of the unclean take a seat in her best room, the infected chair must be removed to the garden to be aired. But did he seat himself in Miss Tyler's own arm-chair, pressing his abominable person into Miss Tyler's own cushion, then passionate were her dismay and despair. To her favourites she was gracious and high-bred, regaling them with reminiscences of Lady Bateman, and with her views on taste, Shakspeare, and the musical glasses. For her little nephew she invented the pretty recreation of pricking playbills; all capital letters were to be illuminated with pin-holes; it was not a boisterous nor an ungenteel sport. At other times the boy would beguile the hours in the garden, making friends with flowers and

insects, or looking wistfully towards that sham castle on
Claverton Hill, seat of romantic mystery, but, alas! two
miles away, and therefore beyond the climbing powers of
a refined gentlewoman.   Southey's hardest daily trial was
the luxurious morning captivity of his aunt's bed; still at
nine, at ten that lady lay in slumber; the small urchin,
long perked up and broad awake, feared by sound or stir
to rouse her, and would nearly wear his little wits away in
plotting re-arrangements of the curtain-pattern, or studying
the motes at mazy play in the slant sunbeam.   His happiest season was when all other little boys were fast asleep;
then, splendid in his gayest "jam," he sat beside Miss Tyler in a front row of the best part of the theatre; when the
yawning fits had passed, he was as open-eyed as the oldest,
and stared on, filling his soul with the spectacle, till the
curtain fell.

The "great red creature," Robert Southey, had now
grown into the lean greyhound of his after-life; his long
legs wanted to be stirring, and there were childish ambitions already at work in his head.   Freedom became dearer to him than the daintiest cage, and when at six he returned to his father's house in Wine Street, it was with
rejoicing.   Now, too, his aunt issued an edict that the
long-legged lad should be breeched; an epoch of life was
complete.   Wine Street, with its freedom, seemed good;
but best of all was a visit to Grandmother Hill's pleasant
house at Bedminster.   "Here I had all wholesome liberty,
all wholesome indulgence, all wholesome enjoyments; and
the delight which I there learnt to take in rural sights and
sounds has grown up with me, and continues unabated to
this day."   And now that scrambling process called education was to begin.   A year was spent by Southey as a
day-scholar with old Mr. Foot, a dissenting minister, whose

unorthodoxy as to the doctrine of the Trinity was in some
measure compensated by sound traditional views as to the
uses of the cane. Mr. Foot, having given proof on the
back of his last and his least pupil of steadfastness in the
faith according to Busby, died; and it was decided that
the boy should be placed under Thomas Flower, who kept
school at Corston, nine miles from Bristol. To a tender
mother's heart nine miles seemed a breadth of severance
cruel as an Atlantic. Mrs. Southey, born to be happy herself, and to make others happy, had always heretofore met
her son with a smile; now he found her weeping in her
chamber; with an effort, such as Southey, man and boy, always knew how to make on like occasions, he gulped down
his own rising sob, and tried to brighten her sorrow with
a smile.

A boy's first night at school is usually not a time of
mirth. The heart of the solitary little lad at Corston
sank within him. A melancholy hung about the decayed
mansion which had once known better days; the broken
gateways, the summer-houses falling in ruins, the grass-
grown court, the bleakness of the schoolroom, ill-disguised
by its faded tapestry, depressed the spirits. Southey's pil-
low was wet with tears before he fell asleep. The master
was at one with his surroundings; he, too, was a piece of
worthy old humanity now decayed; he, too, was falling in
untimely ruins. From the memory of happier days, from
the troubles of his broken fortune, from the vexations of
the drunken maid-servant who was now his wife, he took
refuge in contemplating the order and motions of the
stars. "When he came into his desk, even there he was
thinking of the stars, and looked as if he were out of humour, not from ill-nature, but because his calculations were
interrupted." Naturally the work of the school, such as

it was, fell, for the most part, into the hands of Charley, Thomas Flower's son. Both father and son knew the mystery of that flamboyant penmanship admired by our ancestors, but Southey's handwriting had not yet advanced from the early rounded to the decorated style. His spelling he could look back upon with pride: on one occasion a grand spelling tournament between the boys took place, and little Southey can hardly have failed to overthrow his taller adversaries with the posers, "crystallization" and "coterie." The household arrangements at Corston, as may be supposed, were not of the most perfect kind; Mrs. Flower had so deep an interest in her bottle, and poor Thomas Flower in his planets. The boys each morning washed themselves, or did not, in the brook ankle-deep which ran through the yard. In autumn the brook grew deeper and more swift, and after a gale it would bring within bounds a tribute of floating apples from the neighbouring orchard. That was a merry day, also in autumn, when the boys were employed to pelt the master's walnut-trees; Southey, too small to bear his part in the battery, would glean among the fallen leaves and twigs, inhaling the penetrating fragrance which ever after called up a vision of the brook, the hillside, and its trees. One school-boy sport—that of "conquering" with snail-shells—seems to have been the special invention of Corston. The snail-shells, not tenantless, were pressed point against point until one was broken in. A great conqueror was prodigiously prized, was treated with honourable distinction, and was not exposed to danger save in great emergencies. One who had slain his hundreds might rank with Rodney, to see whom the boys had marched down to the Globe inn, and for whom they had cheered and waved their Sunday cocked hats as he passed by. So, on the whole, life at

Corston had its pleasures. Chief among its pains was the misery of Sunday evenings in winter; then the pupils were assembled in the hall to hear the master read a sermon, or a portion of Stackhouse's *History of the Bible.* "Here," writes Southey, "I sat at the end of a long form, in sight but not within feeling of the fire, my feet cold, my eyelids heavy as lead, and yet not daring to close them — kept awake by fear alone, in total inaction, and under the operation of a lecture more soporific than the strongest sleeping dose." While the boys' souls were thus provided for, there was a certain negligence in matters unspiritual; an alarm got abroad that infection was among them. This hastened the downfall of the school. One night disputing was heard between Charley and his father; in the morning poor Flower was not to be seen, and Charley appeared with a black eye. So came to an end the year at Corston. Southey, aged eight, was brought home, and underwent "a three days' purgatory in brimstone."[1]

What Southey had gained of book-lore by his two years' schooling was as little as could be; but he was already a lover of literature after a fashion of his own. A friend of Miss Tyler had presented him, as soon as he could read, with a series of Newbery's sixpenny books for children — *Goody Twoshoes, Giles Gingerbread,* and the rest — delectable histories, resplendent in Dutch-gilt paper. The true masters of his imagination, however, were the players and playwrights who provided amusement for the pleasure-loving people of Bath. Miss Tyler was acquainted with Colman, and Sheridan, and Cumberland, and Holcroft; her talk

---

[1] Recollections of Corston, somewhat in the manner of Goldsmith's *Deserted Village,* will be found in Southey's early poem, *The Retrospect.*

was of actors and authors, and her nephew soon perceived that, honoured as were both classes, the authors were awarded the higher place. His first dreams of literary fame, accordingly, were connected with the drama. " 'It is the easiest thing in the world to write a play,' said I to Miss Palmer (a friend of Aunt Tyler's), as we were in a carriage on Redcliffe Hill one day, returning from Bristol to Bedminster. 'Is it, my dear?' was her reply. 'Yes,' I continued, 'for you know you have only to think what you would say if you were in the place of the characters, and to make them say it.' " With such a canon of dramatic authorship Southey began a play on the continence of Scipio, and actually completed an act and a half. Shakspeare he read and read again; Beaumont and Fletcher he had gone through before he was eight years old. Were they not great theatrical names, Miss Tyler reasoned, and therefore improving writers for her nephew? and Southey had read them unharmed. When he visited his aunt from Corston, she was a guest with Miss Palmer at Bath; a covered passage led to the playhouse, and every evening the delighted child, seated between the two lady-patronesses of the stage, saw the pageantry and heard the poetry. A little later he persuaded a schoolfellow to write a tragedy; Ballard liked the suggestion, but could not invent a plot. Southey gave him a story; Ballard approved, but found a difficulty in devising names for the *dramatis personæ*. Southey supplied a list of heroic names: they were just what Ballard wanted—but he was at a loss to know what the characters should say. "I made the same attempt," continued Southey, "with another schoolfellow, and with no better success. It seemed to me very odd that they should not be able to write plays as well as to do their lessons."

The ingenious Ballard was an ornament of the school of William Williams, whither Southey was sent as a day-boarder after the catastrophe of Corston. Under the care of this kindly, irascible, little, bewigged old Welshman, Southey remained during four years. Williams was not a model schoolmaster, but he was a man of character and of a certain humorous originality. In two things he believed with all the energy of his nature—in his own spelling-book printed for his own school, and in the Church Catechism. Latin was left to the curate; when Southey reached Virgil, old Williams, delighted with classical attainments rare among his pupils, thought of taking the boy into his own hands, but his little Latin had faded from his brain; and the curate himself seemed to have reached his term in the *Tityre tu patulæ recubans sub tegmine fagi*, so that to Southey, driven round and round the pastoral paddock, the names of Tityrus and Melibœus became for ever after symbols of *ennui*. No prosody was taught: "I am," said Southey, "at this day as liable to make a false quantity as any Scotchman." The credit, however, is due to Williams of having discovered in his favourite pupil a writer of English prose. One day each boy of a certain standing was called upon to write a letter on any subject he pleased: never had Southey written a letter except the formal one dictated at Corston which began with "Honoured Parents." He cried for perplexity and vexation; but Williams encouraged him, and presently a description of Stonehenge filled his slate. The old man was surprised and delighted. A less amiable feeling possessed Southey's schoolfellows: a plan was forthwith laid for his humiliation—could he tell them, fine scholar that he was, what the letters *i. e.* stand for? Southey,

never lacking in courage, drew a bow at a venture : for
John the Evangelist.

The old Welshman, an original himself, had an odd following of friends and poor retainers. There was the crazy
rhymester known as "Dr. Jones;" tradition darkly related
that a dose of cantharides administered by waggish boys
of a former generation had robbed him of his wits. "The
most celebrated *improvisatore* was never half so vain of his
talent as this queer creature, whose little figure of some
five-feet-two I can perfectly call to mind, with his suit of
rusty black, his more rusty wig, and his old cocked hat.
Whenever he entered the schoolroom he was greeted with
a shout of welcome." There was also Pullen, the breeches-
maker—a glorious fellow, brimful of vulgarity, prosperity,
and boisterous good-nature ; above all, an excellent hand
at demanding a half-holiday. A more graceful presence,
but a more fleeting, was that of Mrs. Estan, the actress,
who came to learn from the dancing-master her *minuet de
la cour* in *The Belle's Stratagem.* Southey himself had
to submit to lessons in dancing. Tom Madge, his constant
partner, had limbs that went every way ; Southey's limbs
would go no way : the spectacle presented by their joint
endeavours was one designed for the pencil of Cruikshank.
In the art of reading aloud Miss Tyler had herself instructed her nephew, probably after the manner of the most approved tragedy queens. The grand style did not please
honest Williams. "Who taught you to read?" he asked,
scornfully. "My aunt," answered Southey. "Then give
my compliments to your aunt, and tell her that my old
horse, that has been dead these twenty years, could have
taught you as well "—a message which her nephew, with
the appalling frankness of youth, delivered, and which was
never forgotten.

While Southey was at Corston, his grandmother died; the old lady with the large, clear, brown, bright eyes, seated in her garden, was no more to be seen, and the Bedminster house, after a brief occupation by Miss Tyler, was sold. Miss Tyler spoke of Bristol society with a disdainful sniff; it was her choice to wander for a while from one genteel watering-place to another. When Williams gave Southey his first summer holidays, he visited his aunt at Weymouth. The hours spent there upon the beach were the most spiritual hours of Southey's boyhood; he was for the first time in face of the sea—the sea vast, voiceful, and mysterious. Another epoch-making event occurred about the same time; good Mrs. Dolignon, his aunt's friend, gave him a book—the first which became his very own since that present of the toy-books of Newbery. It was Hoole's translation of Tasso's *Gerusalemme Liberata;* in it a world of poetical adventure was opened to the boy. The notes to Tasso made frequent reference to Ariosto; Bull's Circulating Library at Bath—a Bodleian to Southey —supplied him with the version, also by Hoole, of the *Orlando Furioso;* here was a forest of old romance in which to lose himself. But a greater discovery was to come; searching the notes again, Southey found mention made of Spenser, and certain stanzas of Spenser's chief poem were quoted. "Was the *Faerie Queene* on Bull's shelves?" "Yes," was the answer; "they had it, but it was in obsolete language, and the young gentleman would not understand it." The young gentleman, who had already gone through Beaumont and Fletcher, was not daunted; he fell to with the keenest relish, feeling in Spenser the presence of something which was lacking in the monotonous couplets of Hoole, and charming himself unaware with the music of the stanza.   Spenser, "not more sweet than pure, and not more pure than wise,"

"High-priest of all the Muses' mysteries,"[2]

was henceforth accepted by Southey as his master.

When Miss Tyler had exhausted her friends' hospitality, and had grown tired of lodgings, she settled in a pleasant suburban nook at Bristol; but having a standing quarrel with Thomas Southey, her sister's brother-in-law, she would never set foot in the house in Wine Street, and she tried to estrange her nephew, as far as possible, from his natural home.   Her own brother William, a half-witted creature, she brought to live with her.   "The Squire," as he was called, was hardly a responsible being, yet he had a sort of *half-saved* shrewdness, and a memory stored with old saws, which, says Southey, "would have qualified him, had he been born two centuries earlier, to have worn motley, and figured with a cap and bells and a bauble in some baron's hall."   A saying of his, "Curses are like young chickens, they always come home to roost," was remembered by Southey in after-years; and when it was turned into Greek by Coleridge, to serve as motto to *The Curse of Kehama*, a mysterious reference was given—Αποφθ. Ανεκ. του Γυλίελ. του Μηr.   With much beer-swilling and tobacco-chewing, premature old age came upon him.   He would sit for hours by the kitchen fire, or, on warm days, in the summer-house, his eyes intently following the movements of the neighbours.   He loved to play at marbles with his nephew, and at loo with Miss Tyler; most of all, he loved to be taken to the theatre.   The poor Squire had an affectionate heart; he would fondle children with tenderness, and at

[2] Carmen Nuptiale: Proem, 18.

his mother's funeral his grief was overwhelming. A companion of his own age Southey found in Shadrach Weekes, the boy of all work, a brother of Miss Tyler's maid. Shad and his young master would scour the country in search of violet and cowslip roots, and the bee and fly orchis, until wood and rock by the side of the Avon had grown familiar and had grown dear; and now, instead of solitary pricking of play-bills, Southey set to work, with the help of Shad, to make and fit up such a theatre for puppets as would have been the pride even of Wilhelm Meister.

But fate had already pronounced that Southey was to be poet, and not player. Tasso and Ariosto and Spenser claimed him, or so he dreamed. By this time he had added to his epic cycle Pope's *Homer* and Mickle's *Lusiad*. That prose romance, embroidered with sixteenth-century affectations, but with a true chivalric sentiment at its heart, Sidney's *Arcadia*, was also known to him. He had read Arabian and mock-Arabian tales; he had spent the pocket-money of many weeks on a Josephus, and he had picked up from Goldsmith something of Greek and Roman history. So breathed upon by poetry, and so furnished with erudition, Southey, at twelve years old, found it the most natural thing in the world to become an epic poet. His removal from the old Welshman's school having been hastened by that terrible message which Miss Tyler could not forgive, Southey, before proceeding to Westminster, was placed for a year under a clergyman, believed to be competent to carry his pupils beyond Tityrus and Meliboeus. But, except some skill in writing English themes, little was gained from this new tutor. The year, however, was not lost. " I do not remember," Southey writes, " in any part of my life to have been so conscious of intellectual improvement . . . an improve-

ment derived not from books or instruction, but from
constantly exercising myself in English verse." "Arcadia" was the title of his first dream-poem; it was to
be grafted upon the *Orlando Furioso*, with a new hero,
and in a new scene; this dated from his ninth or tenth
year, and some verses were actually composed. The epic
of the Trojan Brutus and that of King Richard III. were
soon laid aside, but several folio sheets of an *Egbert* came
to be written. The boy's pride and ambition were solitary and shy. One day he found a lady, a visitor of Miss
Tyler's, with the sacred sheets of *Egbert* in her hand; her
compliments on his poem were deeply resented; and he
determined henceforth to write his epics in a private
cipher. Heroic epistles, translations from Latin poetry,
satires, descriptive and moral pieces, a poem in dialogue
exhibiting the story of the Trojan war, followed in rapid
succession; last, a "Cassibelan," of which three books were
completed. Southey, looking back on these attempts,
notices their deficiency in plan, in construction. "It was
long before I acquired this power — not fairly, indeed,
till I was about five or six and thirty; and it was gained
by practice, in the course of which I learnt to perceive
wherein I was deficient."

One day in February, 1788, a carriage rumbled out of
Bath, containing Miss Palmer, Miss Tyler, and Robert
Southey, now a tall, lank boy with high-poised head, brown
curling hair, bright hazel eyes, and an expression of ardour
and energy about the lips and chin. The ladies were on
their way to London for some weeks' diversion, and Robert Southey was on his way to school at Westminster.
For a while he remained an inconvenient appendage of
his aunt's, wearying of the great city, longing for Shad
and the carpentry, and the Gloucester meadows and the

2

Avon cliffs, and the honest eyes and joyous bark of poor Phillis. April the first — ominous morning — arrived; Southey was driven to Dean's Yard; his name was duly entered; his boarding-house determined; his tutor chosen; farewells were said, and he found himself in a strange world, alone.

CHAPTER II.

WESTMINSTER, OXFORD, PANTISOCRACY, AND MARRIAGE.

OF Southey during his four years at Westminster we know little; his fragment of autobiography, having brought him to the school, soon comes to an untimely close; and for this period we possess no letters. But we know that these were years which contributed much to form his intellect and character; we know that they were years of ardour and of toil; and it is certain that now, as heretofore, his advance was less dependent on what pastors and masters did for him than on what he did for himself. The highest scholarship—that which unites precision with breadth, and linguistic science with literary feeling—Southey never attained in any foreign tongue, except perhaps in the Portuguese and the Spanish. Whenever the choice lay between pausing to trace out a law of language, or pushing forward to secure a good armful of miscellaneous facts, Southey preferred the latter. With so many huge structures of his own in contemplation, he could not gather too much material, nor gather it too quickly. Such fortitude as goes to make great scholars he possessed; his store of patience was inexhaustible; but he could be patient only in pursuit of his proper objects. He could never learn a language in regular fashion; the best grammar, he said, was always the

shortest. Southey's acquaintance with Greek never got
beyond that stage at which Greek, like fairy gold, is apt
to slip away of a sudden unless kept steadfastly in view ;
nearly all the Greek he had learnt at Westminster he forgot at Oxford. A monkish legend in Latin of the Church
or a mediæval Latin chronicle he could follow with the run
of the eye ; but had he at any season of his manhood been
called on to write a page of Latin prose, it would probably
have resembled the French in which he sometimes sportive-
ly addressed his friends by letter, and in which he uttered
himself valiantly while travelling abroad.

Southey brought to Westminster an imagination stored
with the marvels and the beauty of old romance. He left
it skilled in the new sentiment of the time—a sentiment
which found in Werther and Eloisa its dialect, high-pitched,
self-conscious, rhapsodical, and not wholly real. His bias
for history was already marked before he entered the
school ; but his knowledge consisted of a few clusters of
historical facts grouped around the subjects of various projected epics, and dotting at wide distances and almost at
random the vast expanse of time. Now he made acquaintance with that book which, more than any other, displays
the breadth, the variety, and the independence of the visible lives of nations. Gibbon's *Decline and Fall* leaves a
reader cold who cares only to quicken his own inmost being by contact with what is most precious in man's spiritual history; one chapter of Augustine's *Confessions*, one
sentence of the *Imitation*—each a live coal from off the
altar—will be of more worth to such an one than all the
mass and laboured majesty of Gibbon. But one who can
gaze with a certain impersonal regard on the spectacle of
the world will find the *Decline and Fall of the Roman Empire*, more than almost any other single book, replenish and

dilate the mind. In it Southey viewed for the first time
the sweep, the splendour, the coils, the mighty movement,
of the stream of human affairs.

Southey's ambition on entering Westminster was to have
the friendship of the youths who had acted in the last
Westminster play, and whose names he had seen in the
newspaper. Vain hope! for they, already preparing to tie
their hair in tails, were looking onward to the great world,
and had no glance to cast on the unnoted figures of the
under-fourth. The new-comer, according to a custom of
the school, was for a time effaced, ceasing to exist as an individual entity, and being known only as "shadow" of the
senior boy chosen to be "substance" to him during his no-
viciate. Southey accepted his effacement the more will-
ingly because George Strachey, his substance, had a good
face and a kindly heart; unluckily—Strachey boarding at
home—they were parted each night. A mild young aris-
tocrat, joining little with the others, was head of the house;
and Southey, unprotected by his chief, stood exposed to
the tyranny of a fellow-boarder bigger and brawnier than
himself, who would souse the ears of his sleeping victim
with water, or on occasions let fly the porter - pot or the
poker at his head. Aspiring beyond these sallies to a
larger and freer style of humour, he attempted one day to
hang Southey out of an upper window by the leg; the
pleasantry was taken ill by the smaller boy, who offered
an effectual resistance, and soon obtained his remove to another chamber. Southey's mature judgment of boarding-
school life was not, on the whole, favourable; yet to Westminster he owed two of his best and dearest possessions—
the friendship of C. W. W. Wynn, whose generous loyalty
alone made it possible for Southey to pursue literature as
his profession, and the friendship, no less precious, of Gros-

venor Bedford, lasting green and fresh from boyhood until
both were white-haired, venerable men.

Southey's interest in boyish sports was too slight to
beguile him from the solitude needful for the growth of
a poet's mind.   He had thoughts of continuing Ovid's
Metamorphoses; he planned six books to complete the
Faery Queen, and actually wrote some cantos; already the
subject of *Madoc* was chosen.   And now a gigantic con-
ception, which at a later time was to bear fruit in such
poems as *Thalaba* and *Kehama*, formed itself in his mind.
"When I was a schoolboy at Westminster," he writes,
"I frequented the house of a schoolfellow who has continued till this day to be one of my most intimate and
dearest friends.   The house was so near Dean's Yard that
it was hardly considered as being out of our prescribed
bounds; and I had free access to the library, a well-stored
and pleasant room . . . looking over the river.   There
many of my truant hours were delightfully spent in reading Picart's *Religious Ceremonies.*   The book impressed
my imagination strongly; and before I left school I had
formed the intention of exhibiting all the more prominent
and poetical forms of mythology, which have at any time
obtained among mankind, by making each the ground-
work of an heroic poem."   Southey's huge design was
begotten upon his *pia mater* by a folio in a library.   A
few years earlier Wordsworth, a boy of fourteen, walking
between Hawkshead and Ambleside, noticed the boughs
and leaves of an oak-tree intensely outlined in black against
a bright western sky.   "That moment," he says, " was
important in my poetical history, for I date from it my
consciousness of the infinite variety of natural appearances
which had been unnoticed by the poets of any age or
country, so far as I was acquainted with them; and I

made a resolution to supply in some degree the deficiency."
Two remarkable incidents in the history of English poetry,
and each with something in it of a typical character.

At Westminster Southey obtained his first literary prof-
its—the guerdon of the silver penny to which Cowper al-
ludes in his *Table-Talk*. Southey's penny — exchanged
for current coin in the proportion of six to one by the
mistress of the boarding-house—was always awarded for
English composition. But his fame among his schoolfellows was not of an early or sudden growth. In the year
of Southey's entrance, some of the senior boys commenced
a weekly paper called *The Trifler*. It imitates, with some
skill, the periodical essay of the post-Johnsonian period :
there is the wide-ranging discussion on the Influence of
Liberty on Genius ; there is the sprightly sketch of Amelia,
a learned Lady ; there is the moral diatribe on Deists, a
Sect of Infidels most dangerous to Mankind ; there are the
letters from Numa and from Infelix ; there is the Eastern
apologue, beginning, " In the city of Bassora lived Zaydor,
the son of Al-Zored." Southey lost no time in sending
to the editor his latest verses ; a baby sister, Margaretta,
had just died, and Southey expressed in elegy a grief which
was real and keen. " The Elegy signed B. is received "—
so Mr. Timothy Touchstone announced on the Saturday
after the manuscript had been dropped into the penny
post. The following Saturday — anxiously expected—
brought no poem, but another announcement : " The Elegy by B. must undergo some Alterations ; a Liberty I
must request all my Correspondents to permit me to take."
" After this," says Southey, " I looked for its appearance
anxiously, but in vain." Happily no one sought to discover B., or supposed that he was one with the curly-head-
ed boy of the under-fourth.

If authorship has its hours of disappointment, it has compensating moments of glory and of joy. *The Trifler*, having lived to the age of ten months, deceased. In 1792 Southey, now a great boy, with Strachey, his sometime "substance," and his friends Wynn and Bedford, planned a new periodical of ill-omened name, *The Flagellant*. " I well remember my feelings," he writes, "when the first number appeared. . . . It was Bedford's writing, but that circumstance did not prevent me from feeling that I was that day borne into the world as an author; and if ever my head touched the stars while I walked upon the earth, it was then. . . . In all London there was not so vain, so happy, so elated a creature as I was that day." From that starry altitude he soon descended. The subject of an early number of *The Flagellant* was flogging; the writer was Robert Southey. He was full of Gibbon at the time, and had caught some of Voltaire's manner of poignant irony. Rather for disport of his wits than in the character of a reformer, the writer of number five undertook to prove from the ancients and the Fathers that flogging was an invention of the devil. During Southey's life the devil received many insults at his hands; his horns, his hoofs, his teeth, his tail, his moral character, were painfully referred to; and the devil took it, like a sensible fiend, in good part. Not so Dr. Vincent; the preceptorial dignity was impugned by some unmannerly brat; a bulwark of the British Constitution was at stake. Dr. Vincent made haste to prosecute the publisher for libel. Matters having taken unexpectedly so serious a turn, Southey came forward, avowed himself the writer, and, with some sense of shame in yielding to resentment so unwarranted and so dull, he offered his apology. The head-master's wrath still held on its way, and Southey was privately expelled.

All Southey's truant hours were not passed among folios
adorned with strange sculptures. In those days even St.
Peter's College, Westminster, could be no little landlocked
bay—silent, secure, and dull. To be in London was to be
among the tides and breakers of the world. Every post
brought news of some startling or significant event. Now
it was that George Washington had been elected first Pres-
ident of the American Republic; now that the States-Gen-
eral were assembled at Versailles; now that Paris, delivered from her nightmare towers of the Bastille, breathed
free; now that Brissot was petitioning for dethronement.
The main issues of the time were such as to try the spirits.
Southey, who was aspiring, hopeful, and courageous, did
not hesitate in choosing a side; a new dawn was opening
for the world, and should not his heart have its portion
in that dawn?

The love of our own household which surrounds us like
the air, and which seems inevitable as our daily meat and
drink, acquires a strange preciousness when we find that
the world can be harsh. The expelled Westminster boy
returned to Bristol, and faithful Aunt Tyler welcomed him
home; Shad did not avert his face, and Phillis looked up
at him with her soft spaniel eyes. But Bristol also had
its troubles; the world had been too strong for the poor
linen-draper in Wine Street; he had struggled to maintain
his business, but without success; his fortune was now
broken, and his heart broke with it. In some respects it
was well for Southey that his father's affairs gave him definite realities to attend to; for, in the quiet and vacancy of
the days in Miss Tyler's house, his heart took unusual heats
and chills, and even his eager verse-writing could not allay
the excitement nor avert the despondent fit. When Michaelmas came, Southey went up to Oxford to matriculate;

C   2*   3

it was intended that he should enter at Christ Church, but
the dean had heard of the escapade at Westminster; there
was a laying of big-wigs together over that adventure, and
the young rebel was rejected; to be received, however, by
Balliol College. But to Southey it mattered little at the
time whether he were of this college or of that; a sum-
mons had reached him to hasten to Bristol that he might
follow his father's body to the grave, and now his thoughts
could not but cling to his mother in her sorrow and her
need.

"I left Westminster," says Southey, "in a perilous state
—a heart full of poetry and feeling, a head full of Rousseau and Werther, and my religious principles shaken by
Gibbon: many circumstances tended to give me a wrong
bias, none to lead me right, except adversity, the whole-
somest of all discipline." The young republican went up
to chambers in Rat Castle—since departed—near the head
of Balliol Grove, prepared to find in Oxford the seat of
pedantry, prejudice, and aristocracy; an airy sense of his
own enlightenment and emancipation possessed him. He
has to learn to pay respect to men "remarkable only for
great wigs and little wisdom." He finds it "rather dis-
graceful at the moment when Europe is on fire with freedom—when man and monarch are contending—to sit and
study Euclid and Hugo Grotius." Beside the enthusiasm
proper in Southey's nature, there was at this time an enthusiasm prepense. He had learnt from his foreign masters
the language of hyper-sensibility; his temperament was
nervous and easily wrought upon; his spirit was generous
and ardent. Like other youths with a facile literary talent
before finding his true self, he created a number of artificial
selves, who uttered for him his moralizings and philoso-
phizings, who declaimed for him on liberty, who dictated

long letters of sentimental platitudes, and who built up
dream - fabrics of social and political reforms, chiefly for
the pleasure of seeing how things might look in "the brilliant colours of fancy, nature, and Rousseau." In this there
was no insincerity, though there was some unreality. "For
life," he says, "I have really a very strong predilection,"
and the buoyant energy within him delayed the discovery
of the bare facts of existence; it was so easy and enjoy-
able to become in turn sage, reformer, and enthusiast. Or
perhaps we ought to say that all this time there was a real
Robert Southey, strong, upright, ardent, simple; and although this was quite too plain a person to serve the pur-
poses of epistolary literature, it was he who gave their cues
to the various ideal personages. This, at least, may be af-
firmed—all Southey's unrealities were of a pure and generous cast; never was his life emptied of truth and meaning,
and made in the deepest degree phantasmal by a secret
shame lurking under a fair show. The youth Milton, with
his grave upbringing, was happily not in the way of catch-
ing the trick of sentimental phrases; but even Milton at
Cambridge, the lady of his College, was not more clean
from spot or blemish than was Southey amid the vulgar
riot and animalisms of young Oxford.

Two influences came to the aid of Southey's instinctive
modesty, and confirmed him in all that was good. One
was his friendship with Edmund Seward, too soon taken
from him by death. The other was his discipleship to a
great master of conduct. One in our own day has acknowledged the largeness of his debt to

> "That halting slave, who in Nicopolis
> Taught Arrian, when Vespasian's brutal son
> Clear'd Rome of what most shamed him."

3

Epictetus came to Southey precisely when such a master
was needed; other writers had affected him through his
imagination, through his nervous sensibility; they had
raised around him a luminous haze; they had plunged
him deeper in illusion. Now was heard the voice of a
conscience speaking to a conscience; the manner of speech
was grave, unfigured, calm; above all, it was real, and the
words bore in upon the hearer's soul with a quiet resist-
lessness. He had allowed his sensitiveness to set up what
excitements it might please in his whole moral frame; he
had been squandering his emotions; he had been indulging in a luxury and waste of passion. Here was a tonic
and a styptic. Had Southey been declamatory about
freedom? The bondsman Epictetus spoke of freedom
also, and of how it might be obtained. Epictetus, like
Rousseau, told of a life according to nature; he commend-
ed simplicity of manners. But Rousseau's simplicity, notwithstanding that homage which he paid to the will, seemed to heat the atmosphere with strange passion, seemed
to give rise to new curiosities and refinements of self-conscious emotion. Epictetus showed how life could be sim-
plified, indeed, by bringing it into obedience to a perfect
law. Instead of a quietism haunted by feverish dreams
— duty, action, co-operation with God. "Twelve years
ago," wrote Southey in 1806, "I carried Epictetus in my
pocket till my very heart was ingrained with it, as a pig's
bones become red by feeding him upon madder. And
the longer I live, and the more I learn, the more am I con-
vinced that Stoicism, properly understood, is the best and
noblest of systems." Much that Southey gained from
Stoicism he kept throughout his whole life, tempered, indeed, by the influences of a Christian faith, but not lost.
He was no metaphysician, and a master who had placed

metaphysics first and morals after would hardly have won
him for a disciple; but a lofty ethical doctrine spoke to
what was deepest and most real in his nature.   To trust
in an over-ruling Providence, to accept the disposal of
events not in our own power with a strenuous loyalty to
our Supreme Ruler, to hold loose by all earthly possessions
even the dearest, to hold loose by life itself while putting
it to fullest use — these lessons he first learnt from the
Stoic slave, and he forgot none of them.   But his chief
lesson was the large one of self - regulation, that it is a
man's prerogative to apply the reason and the will to the
government of conduct and to the formation of character.

By the routine of lectures and examinations Southey
profited little; he was not driven into active revolt, and
that was all.   His tutor, half a democrat, surprised him by
praising America, and asserting the right of every country
to model its own forms of government.   He added, with
a pleasing frankness which deserves to be imitated, "Mr.
Southey, you won't learn anything by my lectures, sir; so,
if you have any studies of your own, you had better pursue them."   Of all the months of his life, those passed
at Oxford, Southey declared, were the most unprofitable.
"All I learnt was a little swimming . . . and a little boat-
ing. . . . I never remember to have dreamt of Oxford—a
sure proof how little it entered into my moral being; of
school, on the contrary, I dream perpetually."   The miscellaneous society of workers, idlers, dunces, bucks, men of
muscle and men of money, did not please him; he lacked
what Wordsworth calls "the congregating temper that
pervades our unripe years."   One or two friends he chose,
and grappled them to his heart; above all, Seward, who
abridged his hours of sleep for sake of study — whose
drink was water, whose breakfast was dry bread; then,

Wynn and Lightfoot.   With Seward he sallied forth, in
the Easter vacation, 1793, for a holiday excursion; passed,
with "the stupidity of a democratic philosopher," the very
walls of Blenheim, without turning from the road to view
the ducal palace; lingered at Evesham, and wandered
through its ruined Abbey, indulging in some passable mediæval romancing; reached Worcester and Kidderminster.
"We returned by Bewdley.   There is an old mansion, once
Lord Herbert's, now mouldering away, in so romantic a
situation, that I soon lost myself in dreams of days of
yore: the tapestried room — the listed fight — the vassal-
filled hall — the hospitable fire — the old baron and his
young daughter — these formed a most delightful day-
dream."   The youthful democrat did not suspect that
such day-dreams were treasonable—a hazardous caressing
of the wily enchantress of the past; in his pocket he carried Milton's *Defence*, which may have been his amulet of
salvation.   Many and various elements could mingle in
young brains a-seethe with revolution and romanticism.
The fresh air and quickened blood at least put Southey
into excellent spirits.   "We must walk over Scotland; it
will be an adventure to delight us all the remainder of
our lives: we will wander over the hills of Morven, and
mark the driving blast, perchance bestrodden by the spirit
of Ossian !"

Among visitors to the Wye, in July, 1793, were William
Wordsworth, recently returned from France, and Robert
Southey, holiday-making from Oxford; they were probably unacquainted with each other at that time even by
name.   Wordsworth has left an undying memorial of his
tour in the poem written near Tintern Abbey, five years
later.   Southey was drawing a long breath before he uttered himself in some thousands of blank verses.   The

father of his friend Bedford resided at Brixton Cause-
way, about four miles on the Surrey side of London; the
smoke of the great city hung heavily beyond an interven-
ing breadth of country; shady lanes led to the neighbouring villages; the garden was a sunny solitude where flowers opened and fruit grew mellow, and bees and birds were
happy. Here Southey visited his friend; his nineteenth
birthday came; on the following morning he planted himself at the desk in the garden summer-house; morning
after morning quickly passed; and by the end of six
weeks *Joan of Arc*, an epic poem in twelve books, was
written. To the subject Southey was attracted primarily
by the exalted character of his heroine; but apart from
this it possessed a twofold interest for him : England, in
1793, was engaged in a war against France—a war hateful
to all who sympathized with the Republic; Southey's epic
was a celebration of the glories of French patriotism, a
narrative of victory over the invader. It was also chivalric and mediæval; the sentiment which was transforming
the word Gothic, from a term of reproach to a word of
vague yet mastering fascination, found expression in the
young poet's treatment of the story of Joan of Arc.
Knight and hermit, prince and prelate, doctors seraphic
and irrefragable with their pupils, meet in it; the castle
and the cathedral confront one another: windows gleam
with many-coloured light streaming through the rich robes
of saint and prophet; a miracle of carven tracery branches
overhead; upon the altar burns the mystic lamp.

The rough draft of *Joan* was hardly laid aside when
Southey's sympathies with the revolutionary movement
in France, strained already to the utmost point of tension,
were fatally rent. All his faith, all his hope, were given
to the Girondin party; and from the Girondins he had

singled out Brissot as his ideal of political courage, purity,
and wisdom. Brissot, like himself, was a disciple of Jean
Jacques; his life was austere; he had suffered on behalf
of freedom. On the day when the Bastille was stormed,
its keys were placed in Brissot's hands; it was Brissot
who had determined that war should be declared against
the foreign foes of the Republic. But now the Girondins
—following hard upon Marie Antoinette — were in the
death-carts; they chanted their last hymn of liberty, ever
growing fainter while the axe lopped head after head; and
Brissot was among the martyrs (October 31, 1793). Probably no other public event so deeply affected Southey. "I
am sick of the world," he writes, "and discontented with
every one in it. The murder of Brissot has completely
harrowed up my faculties. . . . I look round the world,
and everywhere find the same spectacle — the strong tyr-
annizing over the weak, man and beast. . . . There is no
place for virtue."

After this, though Southey did not lose faith in democratic principles, he averted his eyes for a time from
France : how could he look to butchers who had shed
blood which was the very life of liberty, for the realization of his dreams? And whither should he look?
Had he but ten thousand republicans like himself, they
might repeople Greece and expel the Turk. Being but
one, might not Cowley's fancy, a cottage in America, be
transformed into a fact : "three rooms . . . and my only
companion some poor negro whom I have bought on purpose to emancipate?" Meanwhile he occupied a room in
Aunt Tyler's house, and, instead of swinging the axe in
some forest primeval, amused himself with splitting a
wedge of oak in company with Shad, who might, perhaps,
serve for the emancipated negro. Moreover, he was very

diligently driving his quill: "I have finished transcribing *Joan*, and have bound her in marble paper with green ribbons, and am now copying all my remainables to carry to Oxford. Then once more a clear field, and then another epic poem, and then another." Appalling announcement! "I have accomplished a most arduous task, transcribing all my verses that appear worth the trouble, except letters. Of these I took one list—another of my pile of stuff and nonsense — and a third of what I have burnt and lost; upon an average 10,000 verses are burnt and lost; the same number preserved, and 15,000 worthless." Such sad mechanic exercise dulled the ache in Southey's heart; still "the visions of futurity," he finds, "are dark and gloomy, and the only ray that enlivens the scene beams on America."

To Balliol Southey returned; and if the future of the world seemed perplexing, so also did his individual future. His school and college expenses were borne by Mrs. Southey's brother, the Rev. Herbert Hill, chaplain to the British Factory at Lisbon. In him the fatherless youth found one who was both a friend and a father. Holbein's portrait of Sir Thomas More in his best years might have passed for that of Mr. Hill; there was the same benign thoughtfulness in his aspect, the same earnest calm, the same brightness and quietness, the same serene and cheerful strength. He was generous and judicious, learned and modest, and his goodness carried authority with it. Uncle Hill's plan had been that Southey, like himself, should become an English clergyman. But though he might have preached from an Unitarian pulpit, Southey could not take upon himself the vows of a minister of the Church of England. It would have instantly relieved his mother had he entered into orders. He longed that this were possible,

and went through many conflicts of mind, and not a little
anguish. "God knows I would exchange every intellectual gift which He has blessed me with, for implicit faith to
have been able to do this;" but it could not be. To bear
the reproaches, gentle yet grave, of his uncle was hard; to
grieve his mother was harder. Southey resolved to go to
the anatomy school, and fit himself to be a doctor. But
he could not overcome his strong repugnance to the dissecting-room; it expelled him whether he would or no;
and all the time literature, with still yet audible voice, was
summoning him. Might he not obtain some official employment in London, and also pursue his true calling?
Beside the desire of pleasing his uncle and of aiding his
mother, the Stoic of twenty had now a stronger motive
for seeking some immediate livelihood. "I shall joyfully
bid adieu to Oxford," he writes, ". . . and, when I know
my situation, unite myself to a woman whom I have long
esteemed as a sister, and for whom I now indulge a warmer sentiment." But Southey's reputation as a dangerous
Jacobin stood in his way; how could his Oxford overseers
answer for the good behaviour of a youth who spoke
scornfully of Pitt?

The shuttles of the fates now began to fly faster, and
the threads to twist and twine. It was June of the year
1794. A visitor from Cambridge was one day introduced
to Southey; he seemed to be of an age near his own; his
hair, parted in the middle, fell wavy upon his neck; his face,
when the brooding cloud was not upon him, was bright
with an abundant promise — a promise vaguely told in
lines of the sweet full lips, in the luminous eyes, and the
forehead that was like a god's. This meeting of Southey
and Coleridge was an event which decided much in the
careers of both. In the summer days and in youth, the

meeting-time of spirits, they were drawn close to one another. Both had confessions to make, with many points
in common ; both were poets ; both were democrats ; both
had hoped largely from France, and the hopes of both had
been darkened ; both were uncertain what part to take in
life. We do not know whether Coleridge quickly grew
so confidential as to tell of his recent adventure as Silas
Titus Comberbatch of the 15th Light Dragoons. But we
know that Coleridge had a lively admiration for the tall
Oxford student—a person of distinction, so dignified, so
courteous, so quick of apprehension, so full of knowledge,
with a glance so rapid and piercing, with a smile so good
and kind. And we know that Coleridge lost no time in
communicating to Southey the hopes that were nearest to
his heart.

Pantisocracy, word of magic, summed up these hopes.
Was it not possible for a number of men like themselves,
whose way of thinking was liberal, whose characters were
tried and incorruptible, to join together and leave this old
world of falling thrones and rival anarchies, for the woods
and wilds of the young republic ? One could wield an
axe, another could guide a plough. Their wants would be
simple and natural ; their toil need not be such as the
slaves of luxury endure ; where possessions were held in
common, each would work for all ; in their cottages the
best books would have a place ; literature and science,
bathed anew in the invigorating stream of life and nature,
could not but rise reanimated and purified. Each young
man should take to himself a mild and lovely woman for
his wife ; it would be her part to prepare their innocent
food, and tend their hardy and beautiful race. So they
would bring back the patriarchal age, and in the sober
evening of life they would behold "colonies of indepen-

dence in the undivided dale of industry." All the arguments in favour of such a scheme could not be set forth in a conversation, but Coleridge, to silence objectors, would publish a quarto volume on Pantisocracy and Aspheterism.

Southey heartily assented; his own thoughts had, with a vague forefeeling, been pointing to America; the unpublished epic would serve to buy a spade, a plough, a few acres of ground; he could assuredly split timber; he knew a mild and lovely woman for whom he indulged a warmer sentiment than that of a brother. Robert Lovell, a Quaker, an enthusiast, a poet, married to the sister of Southey's Edith, would surely join them; so would Burnett, his college friend; so, perhaps, would the admirable Seward. The long vacation was at hand. Being unable to take orders, or to endure the horrors of the dissecting-room, Southey must no longer remain a burden upon his uncle; he would quit the university and prepare for the voyage.

Coleridge departed to tramp it through the romantic valleys and mountains of Wales. Southey joined his mother, who now lived at Bath, and her he soon persuaded— as a handsome and eloquent son can persuade a loving mother — that the plan of emigration was feasible; she even consented to accompany her boy. But his aunt— an *esprit borné*—was not to hear a breath of Pantisocracy; still less would it be prudent to confess to her his engagement to Miss Edith Fricker. His Edith was penniless, and therefore all the dearer to Southey; her father had been an unsuccessful manufacturer of sugar-pans. What would Miss Tyler, the friend of Lady Bateman, feel? What words, what gestures, what acts, would give her feelings relief?

When Coleridge, after his Welsh wanderings, arrived in Bristol, he was introduced to Lovell, to Mrs. Lovell, to Mrs.

Lovell's sisters, Edith and Sarah, and Martha and Elizabeth.
Mrs. Lovell was doubtless already a pantisocrat; Southey
had probably not found it difficult to convert Edith; Sarah,
the elder sister, who was wont to look a mild reproof on
over-daring speculations, seriously inclined to hear of pantisocracy from the lips of Coleridge. All members of the
community were to be married. Coleridge now more than
ever saw the propriety of that rule; he was prepared to
yield obedience to it with the least possible delay. Burnett, also a pantisocrat, must also marry. Would Miss
Martha Fricker join the community as Mrs. George Burnett? The lively little woman refused him scornfully; if
he wanted a wife in a hurry, let him go elsewhere. The
prospects of the reformers, this misadventure notwithstanding, from day to day grew brighter. "This Pantisocratic
scheme," so writes Southey, "has given me new life, new
hope, new energy; all the faculties of my mind are dilated."
Coleridge met a friend of Priestley's. But a few days
since he had toasted the great doctor at Bala, thereby calling forth a sentiment from the loyal parish apothecary: "I
gives a sentiment, gemmen! May all republicans be gullo-
teened!" The friend of Priestley's said that without doubt
the doctor would join them. An American land-agent told
them that for twelve men 2000*l.* would do. "He recom-
mends the Susquehanna, from its excessive beauty and its
security from hostile Indians." The very name—Susquehanna—sounded as if it were the sweetest of rippling rivers. Money, it is true, as Southey admits, "is a huge evil;"
but now they are twenty-seven, and by resolute men this
difficulty can be overcome.

It was evening of the 17th of October, a dark and gusty
evening of falling rain and miry ways. Within Aunt Tyler's house in College Green, Bristol, a storm was burst-

ing ; she had heard it all at last—Pantisocracy, America,
Miss Fricker. Out of the house he must march; there
was the door; let her never see his face again. Southey
took his hat, looked for the last time in his life at his aunt,
then stepped out into the darkness and the rain. "Why,
sir, you ben't going to Bath at this time of night and in
this weather?" remonstrated poor Shadrach. Even so ; and
with a friendly whisper master and man parted. Southey
had not a penny in his pocket, and was lightly clad. At
Lovell's he luckily found his father's great-coat; he swal-
lowed a glass of brandy and set off on foot. Misery makes
one acquainted with strange road-fellows. On the way he
came upon an old man, drunk, and hardly able to stumble
forward through the night: the young pantisocrat, mind-
ful of his fellow-man, dragged him along nine miles amid
rain and mire. Then, with weary feet, he reached Bath,
and there was his mother to greet him with surprise, and
to ask for explanations. " Oh, Patience, Patience, thou
hast often helped poor Robert Southey, but never didst
thou stand him in more need than on Friday, the 17th of
October, 1794."

For a little longer the bow of hope shone in the West,
somewhere over the Susquehanna, and then it gradually
grew faint and faded. Money, that huge evil, sneered its
cold negations. The chiefs consulted, and Southey proposed that a house and farm should be taken in Wales,
where their principles might be acted out until better days
enabled them to start upon their voyage. One pantisocrat,
at least, could be happy with Edith, brown bread, and wild
Welsh raspberries. But Coleridge objected ; their principles could not be fairly tested under the disadvantage of
an effete and adverse social state surrounding them ; besides, where was the purchase-money to come from ? how

were they to live until the gathering of their first crops?
It became clear that the realization of their plan must be
postponed. The immediate problem was, How to raise
150*l.*? With such a sum they might both qualify by marriage for membership in the pantisocratical community.
After that, the rest would somehow follow.

How, then, to raise 150*l.*? Might they not start a new
magazine and become joint editors? The *Telegraph* had
offered employment to Southey. "Hireling writer to a
newspaper! 'Sdeath! 'tis an ugly title; but *n'importe.*
I shall write truth, and only truth." The offer, however,
turned out to be that of a reporter's place; and his trou-
blesome guest, honesty, prevented his contributing to *The
True Briton.* But he and Coleridge could at least write
poetry, and perhaps publish it with advantage to themselves; and they could lecture to a Bristol audience. With
some skirmishing lectures on various political subjects of
immediate interest, Coleridge began; many came to hear
them, and the applause was loud. Thus encouraged, he
announced and delivered two remarkable courses of lectures—one, *A Comparative View of the English Rebellion
under Charles I. and the French Revolution;* the other,
*On Revealed Religion: its Corruptions and its Political
Views.* Southey did not feel tempted to discuss the origin
of evil or the principles of revolution. He chose as his
subject a view of the course of European history from
Solon and Lycurgus to the American War. His hearers
were pleased by the graceful delivery and unassuming self-
possession of the young lecturer, and were quick to recognize the unusual range of his knowledge, his just perception
of facts, his ardour and energy of conviction. One lecture
Coleridge begged permission to deliver in Southey's place
—that on the Rise, Progress, and Decline of the Roman

Empire. Southey consented, and the room was thronged; but no lecturer appeared; they waited; still no lecturer. Southey offered an apology, and the crowd dispersed in no happy temper. It is likely, adds that good old gossip Cottle, who tells the story, "that at this very moment Mr. Coleridge might have been found at No. 48 College Street, composedly smoking his pipe, and lost in profound musings on his divine Susquehanna."

The good Cottle—young in 1795, a publisher, and unhappily a poet—rendered more important service to the two young men than that of smoothing down their ruffled tempers after this incident. Southey, in conjunction with Lovell, had already published a slender volume of verse. The pieces by Southey recall his schoolboy joys and sorrows, and tell of his mother's tears, his father's death, his friendship with "Urban," his love of "Ariste," lovely maid! his delight in old romance, his discipleship to Rousseau. They are chiefly of interest as exhibiting the diverse literary influences to which a young writer of genius was exposed in the last quarter of the eighteenth century. Here the couplet of Pope reappears, and hard by the irregular ode as practised by Akenside, the elegy as written by Gray, the unrhymed stanza which Collins's *Evening* made a fashion, the sonnet to which Bowles had lent a meditative grace, and the rhymeless measures imitated by Southey from Sayers, and afterwards made popular by his *Thalaba*. On the last page of this volume appear " Proposals for publishing by subscription *Joan of Arc ;*" but subscriptions came slowly in. One evening Southey read for Cottle some books of *Joan*. " It can rarely happen," he writes, " that a young author should meet with a bookseller as inexperienced and as ardent as himself." Cottle offered to publish the poem in quarto, to make it the handsomest

book ever printed in Bristol, to give the author fifty copies
for his subscribers, and fifty pounds to put forthwith into
his purse.   Some dramatic attempts had recently been
made by Southey, *Wat Tyler*, of which we shall hear
more at a later date, and the *Fall of Robespierre*, undertaken by Coleridge, Lovell, and Southey, half in sport—
each being pledged to produce an act in twenty-four
hours.   These were now forgotten, and all his energies
were given to revising and in part recasting *Joan*.   In
six weeks his epic had been written; its revision occupied
six months.

With summer came a great sorrow, and in the end of
autumn a measureless joy.   "He is dead," Southey writes,
"my dear Edmund Seward! after six weeks' suffering. . . .
You know not, Grosvenor, how I loved poor Edmund: he
taught me all that I have of good. . . . There is a strange
vacancy in my heart. . . . I have lost a friend, and such
a one!"   And then characteristically come the words:
"I will try, by assiduous employment, to get rid of very
melancholy thoughts."   Another consolation Southey possessed: during his whole life he steadfastly believed that
death is but the removal of a spirit from earth to heaven;
and heaven for him meant a place where cheerful familiarity was natural, where, perhaps, he himself would write
more epics and purchase more folios.   As Baxter expected
to meet among the saints above Mr. Hampden and Mr. Pym,
so Southey counted upon the pleasure of having long talks
with friends, of obtaining introductions to eminent strangers; above all, he looked forward to the joy of again em-
bracing his beloved ones:

> "Often together have we talked of death;
>   How sweet it were to see
>   All doubtful things made clear;

> How sweet it were with powers
>   Such as the Cherubim
> To view the depth of Heaven!
>   O Edmund! thou hast first
> Begun the travel of eternity."

Autumn brought its happiness pure and deep. Mr. Hill
had arrived from Lisbon; once again he urged his nephew
to enter the church; but for one of Southey's opinions the
church-gate "is perjury," nor does he even find church-go-
ing the best mode of spending his Sunday. He proposed
to choose the law as his profession. But his uncle had
heard of Pantisocracy, Aspheterism, and Miss Fricker, and
said the law could wait; he should go abroad for six months,
see Spain and Portugal, learn foreign languages, read foreign poetry and history, rummage among the books and
manuscripts his uncle had collected in Lisbon, and afterwards return to his Blackstone. Southey, straightforward
in all else, in love became a Machiavel. To Spain and
Portugal he would go; his mother wished it; Cottle expected from him a volume of travels; his uncle had but
to name the day. Then he sought Edith, and asked her
to promise that before he departed she would become his
wife: she wept to think that he was going, and yet persuaded him to go; consented, finally, to all that he proposed. But how was he to pay the marriage fees and buy
the wedding-ring? Often this autumn he had walked the
streets dinnerless, no pence in his pocket, no bread and
cheese at his lodgings, thinking little, however, of dinner,
for his head was full of poetry and his heart of love. Cottle lent him money for the ring and the license — and
Southey in after-years never forgot the kindness of his
honest friend. He was to accompany his uncle, but Edith
was first to be his own; so she may honourably accept

from him whatever means he can furnish for her support. It was arranged with Cottle's sisters that she should live with them, and still call herself by her maiden name.   On the morning of the 14th of November, 1795—a day sad, yet with happiness underlying all sadness—Robert Southey was married in Redcliffe Church, Bristol, to Edith Fricker. At the church door there was a pressure of hands, and they parted with full hearts, silently—Mrs. Southey to take up her abode in Bristol, with the wedding-ring upon her breast, her husband to cross the sea.   Never did woman put her happiness in more loyal keeping.

So by love and by poetry, by Edith Fricker and by Joan of Arc, Southey's life was being shaped.   Powers most benign leaned forward to brood over the coming years and to bless them.   It was decreed that his heart should be no homeless wanderer; that, as seasons went by, children should be in his arms and upon his knees : it was also decreed that he should become a strong toiler among books.   Now Pantisocracy looked faint and far ; the facts plain and enduring of the actual world took hold of his adult spirit.   And Coleridge complained of this, and did not come to bid his friend farewell.

CHAPTER III.

THROUGH pastoral Somerset, through Devon amid falling leaves, then over rough Cornish roads, the coach brought Southey—cold, hungry, and dispirited—to Falmouth. No packet there for Corunna; no packet starting before December 1st. The gap of time looked colourless and dreary, nor could even the philosophy of Epictetus lift him quite above "the things independent of the will." After a comfortless and stormy voyage, on the fifth morning the sun shone, and through a mist the barren cliffs of Galicia, with breakers tumbling at their feet, rose in sight. Who has not experienced, when first he has touched a foreign soil, how nature purges the visual nerve with lucky euphrasy? The shadowy streets, the latticed houses, the fountains, the fragments of Moorish architecture, the Jewish faces of the men, the lustrous eyes of girls, the children gaily bedizened, the old witch-like women with brown shrivelled parchment for skin, told Southey that he was far from home. Nor at night was he permitted to forget his whereabouts; out of doors cats were uttering soft things in most vile Spanish; beneath his blanket, familiars, bloodthirsty as those of the Inquisition, made him their own. He was not sorry when the crazy coach, drawn by six mules, received him and his uncle, and the journey eastward began to the shout of the muleteers and the clink of a hundred bells.

Some eighteen days were spent upon the road to Madrid. Had Southey not left half his life behind him in Bristol, those December days would have been almost wholly pleasurable. As it was, they yielded a large possession for the inner eye, and gave his heart a hold upon this new land which, in a certain sense, became for ever after the land of his adoption. It was pleasant when, having gone forward on foot, he reached the crest of some mountain road, to look down on broken waters in the glen, and across to the little white-walled convent amid its chestnuts, and back to the dim ocean ; there, on the summit, to rest with the odour of furze blossoms and the tinkle of goats in the air, and, while the mules wound up the long ascent, to turn all this into hasty rhymes, ending with the thought of peace, and love, and Edith. Then the bells audibly approaching, and the loud-voiced muleteer consigning his struggling team to Saint Michael and three hundred devils; and then on to remoter hills, or moor and swamp, or the bridge flung across a ravine, or the path above a precipice, with mist and moonlight below. And next day some walled city, with its decaying towers and dim piazza ; some church, with its balcony of ghastly skulls ; some abandoned castle, or jasper-pillared Moorish gateway and gallery. Nor were the little inns and baiting-houses without compensations for their manifold discomforts. The Spanish country-folk were dirty and ignorant, but they had a courtesy unknown to English peasants ; Southey would join the group around the kitchen fire, and be, as far as his imperfect speech allowed, one with the rustics, the carriers, the hostess, the children, the village barber, the familiar priest, and the familiar pigs. When chambermaid Jo-

sepha took hold of his hair and gravely advised him never
to tie it or to wear powder, she meant simple friendliness,
no more. In his recoil from the dream of human perfec-
tibility, Southey allowed himself at times to square accounts with common-sense by a cynical outbreak; but, in
truth, he was a warm-hearted lover of his kind. Even feu-
dalism and Catholicism had not utterly degraded the Spaniard. Southey thanks God that the pride of chivalry is
extinguished; his Protestant zeal becomes deep - dyed in
presence of our Lady of Seven Sorrows and the Holy
Napkin. "Here, in the words of Mary Wollstonecraft,"
he writes, "'the serious folly of Superstition stares every
man of sense in the face.'" Yet Spain has inherited tender and glorious memories; by the river Ezla he recalls
Montemayor's wooing of his Diana; at Tordesillas he
muses on the spot where Queen Joanna watched by her
husband's corpse, and where Padilla, Martyr of Freedom,
triumphed and endured. At length the travellers, accompanied by Manuel, the most vivacious and accomplished of
barbers, drew near Madrid, passed the miles of kneeling
washerwomen and outspread clothes on the river banks,
entered the city, put up at the Cruz de Malta, and were
not ill-content to procure once more a well-cooked supper
and a clean bed.

Southey pursued with ardour his study of the Spanish
language, and could soon talk learnedly of its great writers.
The national theatres, and the sorry spectacle of bullock-
teasing, made a slighter impression upon him than did the
cloisters of the new Franciscan Convent. He had been
meditating his design of a series of poems to illustrate the
mythologies of the world; here the whole portentous history of St. Francis was displayed upon the walls. "Do
they believe all this, sir?" he asked Mr. Hill. "Yes, and

a great deal more of the same kind," was the reply. " My
first thought was . . . here is a mythology not less wild
and fanciful than any of those upon which my imagination was employed, and one which ought to be included
in my ambitious design." Thus Southey's attention was
drawn for the first time to the legendary and monastic
history of the Church.

His Majesty of Spain, with his courtesans and his cour-
tiers, possibly also with the Queen and her gallants, had
gone westward to meet the Portuguese court upon the
borders. As a matter of course, therefore, no traveller
could hope to leave Madrid, every carriage, cart, horse, mule,
and ass being embargoed for the royal service. The fol-
lowers of the father of his people numbered seven thousand, and they advanced, devouring all before them, neither
paying nor promising to pay, leaving a broad track behind
as bare as that stripped by an army of locusts, with here
a weeping cottager, and there a smoking cork-tree, for a
memorial of their march. Ten days after the king's departure, Mr. Hill and his nephew succeeded in finding a
buggy with two mules, and made their escape, taking with
them their own larder. Their destination was Lisbon, and
as they drew towards the royal party, the risk of embargo
added a zest to travel hardly less piquant than that imparted by the neighbourhood of bandits. It was mid-January ;
the mountains shone with snow ; but olive-gathering had
begun in the plains ; violets were in blossom, and in the
air was a genial warmth. As they drove south and west,
the younger traveller noted for his diary the first appearance of orange - trees, the first myrtle, the first fence of
aloes. A pressure was on their spirits till Lisbon should
be reached ; they would not linger to watch the sad procession attending a body uncovered upon its bier ; they

left behind the pilgrims to our Lady's Shrine, pious bac-
chanals half naked and half drunk, advancing to the tune
of bagpipe and drum; then the gleam of waters before
them, a rough two hours' passage, and the weary heads
were on their pillows, to be roused before morning by an
earthquake, with its sudden trembling and cracking.

Life at Lisbon was not altogether after Southey's heart.
His uncle's books and manuscripts were indeed a treasure
to explore, but Mr. Hill lived in society as well as in his
study, and thought it right to give his nephew the advantage of new acquaintances. What had the author of *Joan
of Arc*, the husband of Edith Southey, the disciple of
Rousseau, of Godwin, the Stoic, the tall, dark-eyed young
man with a certain wildness of expression in his face,
standing alone or discoursing earnestly on Industrial Com-
munities of Women—what had he to do with the *inania
regna* of the drawing-room? He cared not for cards nor
for dancing; he possessed no gift for turning the leaves
on the harpsichord, and saying the happy word at the
right moment. Southey, indeed, knew as little as possible
of music; and all through his life acted on the principle
that the worthiest use of sound without sense had been
long ago discovered by schoolboys let loose from their
tasks; he loved to create a chaos of sheer noise after those
hours during which silence had been interrupted only by
the scraping of his pen. For the rest, the sallies of glee
from a mountain brook, the piping of a thrush from the
orchard-bough, would have delighted him more than all
the trills of Sontag or the finest rapture of Malibran. It
was with some of the superiority and seriousness of a
philosopher just out of his teens that he unbent to the
frivolities of the Lisbon drawing-rooms.

But if Lisbon had its vexations, the country, the climate,

the mountains with their streams and coolness, the odorous gardens, Tagus flashing in the sunlight, the rough bar glittering with white breakers, and the Atlantic, made amends. When April came, Mr. Hill moved to his house at Cintra, and the memories and sensations "felt in the blood and felt along the heart," which Southey brought with him to England, were especially associated with this delightful retreat. "Never was a house more completely secluded than my uncle's: it is so surrounded with lemon-trees and laurels as nowhere to be visible at the distance of ten yards. . . . A little stream of water runs down the hill before the door, another door opens into a lemon-garden, and from the sitting-room we have just such a prospect over lemon-trees and laurels to an opposite hill as, by promising a better, invites us to walk. . . . On one of the mountain eminences stands the Penha Convent, visible from the hills near Lisbon. On another are the ruins of a Moorish castle, and a cistern, within its boundaries, kept always full by a spring of purest water that rises in it. From this elevation the eye stretches over a bare and melancholy country to Lisbon on the one side, and on the other to the distant Convent of Mafra, the Atlantic bounding the greater part of the prospect. I never beheld a view that so effectually checked the wish of wandering."

"Lisbon, from which God grant me a speedy deliverance," is the heading of one of Southey's letters; but when the day came to look on Lisbon perhaps for the last time, his heart grew heavy with happy recollection. It was with no regretful feeling, however, that he leaped ashore, glad, after all, to exchange the sparkling Tagus and the lemon groves of Portugal for the mud-encumbered tide of Avon and a glimpse of British smoke. "I intend to write a hymn," he says, "to the Dii Penates." His joy

3*

in reunion with his wife was made more rare and tender
by finding her in sorrow; the grief was also peculiarly his
own—Lovell was dead. He had been taken ill at Salis-
bury, and by his haste to reach his fireside had heightened
the fever which hung upon him. Coleridge, writing to
his friend Poole at this time, expresses himself with amiable but inactive piety: "The widow is calm, and amused
with her beautiful infant. We are all become more religious than we were. God be ever praised for all things."
Southey also writes characteristically: "Poor Lovell! I
am in hopes of raising something for his widow by publishing his best pieces, if only enough to buy her a harpsichord. . . . Will you procure me some subscribers?"
No idle conceit of serving her; for Mrs. Lovell with her
child, as well as Mrs. Coleridge with her children, at a
later time became members of the Southey household.
Already—though Coleridge might resent it—Southey was
willing to part with some vague enthusiasms which wan·
dered in the inane of a young man's fancy, for the sake
of simple loyalties and manly tendernesses. No one was
more boyish-hearted than Southey at fifty; but even at
twenty-two it would not have been surprising to find grey
hairs sprinkling the dark. "How does time mellow down
our opinions! Little of that ardent enthusiasm which so
lately fevered my whole character remains. I have contracted my sphere of action within the little circle of my
own friends, and even my wishes seldom stray beyond
it. . . . I want a little room to arrange my books in, and
some Lares of my own." This domestic feeling was not
a besotted contentment in narrow interests; no man was
more deeply moved by the political changes in his own
country, by the national uprising in the Spanish peninsula,
than Southey. While seated at his desk, his intellect ranged

through dim centuries of the past.   But his heart needed
an abiding-place, and he yielded to the bonds—strict and
dear—of duty and of love which bound his own life to
the lives of others.

The ambitious quarto on which Cottle prided himself
not a little was now published (1796).   To assign its true
place to *Joan of Arc*, we must remember that narrative
poetry in the eighteenth century was of the slenderest
dimensions and the most modest temper.   Poems of
description and sentiment seemed to leave no place for
poems of action and passion.   Delicately finished cabinet
pictures, like Shenstone's *Schoolmistress* and Goldsmith's
Deserted Village, had superseded fresco.   The only great
English epic of that century is the prose Odyssey of which
Mr. Tom Jones is the hero.   That estimable London mer-
chant, Glover, had indeed written an heroic poem containing the correct number of Books ; its subject was a lofty
one; the sentiments were generous, the language dignified ; and inasmuch as Leonidas was a patriot and a Whig,
true Whigs and patriots bought and praised the poem.
But Glover's poetry lacks the informing breath of life.
His second poem, *The Athenaid*, appeared after his death,
and its thirty books fell plumb into the water of oblivion.
It looked as if the narrative poem *à longue haleine* was
dead in English literature.   Cowper had given breadth,
with a mingled gaiety and gravity, to the poetry of description and sentiment; Burns had made the air tremu-
lous with snatches of pure and thrilling song; the *Lyrical
Ballads* were not yet.   At this moment, from a provincial press, *Joan of Arc* was issued.   As a piece of romantic narrative it belongs to the new age of poetry ; in sentiment it is revolutionary and republican ; its garment of
style is of the eighteenth century.   Nowhere, except it be

in the verses which hail "Inoculation, lovely Maid!" does the personified abstraction, galvanized into life by printer's type and poet's epithet, stalk more at large than in the unfortunate ninth book, the Vision of the Maid, which William Taylor, of Norwich, pronounced worthy of Dante. The critical reviews of the time were liberal in politics, and the poem was praised and bought. "Brissot murdered" was good, and "the blameless wife of Roland" atoned for some offences against taste; there was also that notable reference to the "Almighty people" who "from their tyrant's hand dashed down the iron rod." The delegated maid is a creature overflowing with Rousseauish sensibility; virtue, innocence, the peaceful cot, stand over against the wars and tyranny of kings, and the superstition and cruelty of prelates. Southey himself soon disrelished the youthful heats and violences of the poem; he valued it as the work which first lifted him into public view; and, partly out of a kind of gratitude, he rehandled the *Joan* again and again. It would furnish an instructive lesson to a young writer to note how its asperities were softened, its spasm subdued, its swelling words abated. Yet its chief interest will be perceived only by readers of the earlier text. To the second book Coleridge contributed some four hundred lines, where Platonic philosophy and protests against the Newtonian hypothesis of æther are not very appropriately brought into connexion with the shepherd-girl of Domremi. These lines disappeared from all editions after the first.[1]

---

[1] I find in a Catalogue of English Poetry, 1862, the following passage from an autograph letter of S. T. Coleridge, dated Bristol, July 16, 1814, then in Mr. Pickering's possession: "I looked over the first five books of the first (quarto) edition of *Joan of Arc* yesterday, at Hood's request, in order to mark the lines written by me.

The neighbourhood of Bristol was for the present
Southey's home. The quickening of his blood by the
beauty, the air and sun, of Southern Europe, the sense
of power imparted by his achievement in poetry, the joy
of reunion with his young wife, the joy, also, of solitude
among rocks and woods, combined to throw him into a
vivid and creative mood. His head was full of designs
for tragedies, epics, novels, romances, tales — among the
rest, "My Oriental poem of The Destruction of the Dom
Daniel." He has a "Helicon kind of dropsy" upon him;
he had rather leave off eating than poetizing. He was
also engaged in making the promised book of travel for
Cottle; in what leisure time remained after these employ-
ments he scribbled for *The Monthly Magazine*, and to
good purpose, for in eight months he had earned no less
than "seven pounds and two pair of breeches," which, as
he observes to his brother Tom, "is not amiss." He was
resolved to be happy, and he was happy. Now, too, the
foolish estrangement on Coleridge's part was brought to
an end. Southey had been making some acquaintance
with German literature at second hand. He had read
Taylor's rendering of Bürger's *Lenore*, and wondered who
this William Taylor was; he had read Schiller's *Cabal and
Love* in a wretched translation, finding the fifth act dreadfully affecting; he had also read Schiller's *Fiesco*. Coleridge was just back after a visit to Birmingham, but still

---

I was really astonished—1, at the schoolboy, wretched allegoric ma-
chinery; 2, at the transmogrification of the fanatic Virago into a
modern Novel-pawing proselyte of the Age of Reason, a Tom Paine
in petticoats, but so lovely! and in love more dear! '*On her rubied
cheek hung pity's crystal gem,*' 3, at the utter want of all rhythm in
the verse, the monotony and the dead plumb down of the pauses, and
of the absence of all bone, muscle, and sinew in the single lines."

held off from his brother-in-law and former friend. A
sentence from Schiller, copied on a slip of paper by Southey, with a word or two of conciliation, was sent to the
offended Abdiel of Pantisocracy: "Fiesco! Fiesco! thou
leavest a void in my bosom, which the human race, thrice
told, will never fill up." It did not take much to melt the
faint resentment of Coleridge, and to open his liberal heart.
An interview followed, and in an hour's time, as the story
is told by Coleridge's nephew, "these two extraordinary
youths were arm in arm again."

Seven pounds and two pair of breeches are not amiss,
but pounds take to themselves wings, and fly away: a
poet's wealth is commonly in the *paulo-post-futurum*
tense; it therefore behoved Southey to proceed with his
intended study of the law. By Christmas he would receive the first instalment of an annual allowance of 160*l.*
promised by his generous friend Wynn upon coming of
age; but Southey, who had just written his *Hymn to the
Penates*—a poem of grave tenderness and sober beauty—
knew that those deities are exact in their demand for the
dues of fire and salt, for the firstlings of fruits, and for of-
ferings of fine flour. A hundred and sixty pounds would
not appease them. To London, therefore, he must go, and
Blackstone must become his counsellor. But never did
Sindbad suffer from the tyrannous old man between his
shoulders as Robert Southey suffered from Blackstone.
London in itself meant deprivation of all that he most
cared for; he loved to shape his life in large and simple
lines, and London seemed to scribble over his consciousness with distractions and intricacies. "My spirits always
sink when I approach it. Green fields are my delight.
I am not only better in health, but even in heart, in the
country." Some of his father's love of rural sights and

sounds was in him, though hare-hunting was not an amusement of Southey the younger; he was as little of a sportsman as his friend Sir Thomas More: the only murderous
sport, indeed, which Southey ever engaged in was that of
pistol-shooting, with sand for ammunition, at the wasps in
Bedford's garden, when he needed a diversion from the wars
of Talbot and the "missioned Maid." Two pleasures of
a rare kind London offered—the presence of old friends,
and the pursuit of old books upon the stalls. But not
even for these best lures proposed by the Demon of the
place would Southey renounce

> " The genial influences
> And thoughts and feelings to be found where'er
> We breathe beneath the open sky, and see
> Earth's liberal bosom."

To London, however, he would go, and would read nine
hours a day at law. Although he pleaded at times against
his intended profession, Southey really made a strenuous
effort to overcome his repugnance to legal studies, and for
a while Blackstone and *Madoc* seemed to advance side by
side. But the bent of his nature was strong. " I commit wilful murder on my own intellect," he writes, two
years later, " by drudging at law." And the worst or the
best of it was that all his drudgery was useless. Southey's
memory was of that serviceable, sieve-like kind which re-
tains everything needful to its possessor, and drops everything which is mere incumbrance. Every circumstance in
the remotest degree connected with the seminary of ma-
gicians in the Dom Daniel under the roots of the sea ad-
hered to his memory, but how to proceed in the Court of
Common Pleas was always just forgotten since yesterday.
" I am not indolent: I loathe indolence: but, indeed, read-

ing law is laborious indolence—it is thrashing straw. . . .
I have given all possible attention, and attempted to command volition ; . . . close the book and all was gone." In
1801 there was a chance of Southey's visiting Sicily as
secretary to some Italian Legation. " It is unfortunate,"
he writes to Bedford, " that you cannot come to the sacrifice of one law-book—my whole proper stock—whom I
design to take up to the top of Mount Etna, for the express purpose of throwing him straight to the devil. Huz-
za, Grosvenor ! I was once afraid that I should have a dead-
ly deal of law to forget whenever I had done with it ; but
my brains, God bless them, never received any, and I am as
ignorant as heart could wish. The tares would not grow."

As spring advanced, impatience quickened within him ;
the craving for a lonely place in sight of something green
became too strong. Why might not law be read in Hampshire under blue skies, and also poetry be written ? Southey longed to fill his eyesight with the sea, and with sun-
sets over the sea ; he longed to renew that delicious shock
of plunging in salt waves which he had last enjoyed in the
Atlantic at the foot of the glorious Arrabida mountain.
Lodgings were found at Burton, near Christ Church (1797) ;
and here took place a little Southey family-gathering, for
his mother joined them, and his brother Tom, the mid-
shipman, just released from a French prison. Here, too,
came Cottle, and there were talks about the new volume
of shorter poems. Here came Lloyd, the friend of Coleridge, himself a writer of verse ; and with Lloyd came
Lamb, the play of whose letters show that he found in
Southey not only a fellow-lover of quaint books, but also
a ready smiler at quips and cranks and twinklings of sly
absurdity. And here he found John Rickman, " the stur-
diest of jovial companions," whose clear head and stout

heart were at Southey's service whenever they were needed through all the future years.

When the holiday at Burton was at an end Southey
had for a time no fixed abode. He is now to be seen
roaming over the cliffs by the Avon, and now casting a
glance across some book-stall near Gray's Inn. In these
and subsequent visits to London he was wistful for home,
and eager to hasten back. "At last, my dear Edith, I sit
down to write to you in quiet and something like comfort. . . . My morning has been spent pleasantly, for it has
been spent alone in the library; the hours so employed
pass rapidly enough, but I grow more and more homesick, like a spoilt child. On the 29th you may expect me.
Term opens on the 26th. After eating my third dinner, I
can drive to the mail, and thirteen shillings will be well
bestowed in bringing me home four-and-twenty hours earlier: it is not above sixpence an hour, Edith, and I would
gladly purchase an hour at home now at a much higher
price."

A visit to Norwich (1798) was pleasant and useful, as
widening the circle of his literary friends. Here Southey
obtained an introduction to William Taylor, whose translations from the German had previously attracted his notice. Norwich, at the end of the last century and the beginning of the present, was a little Academe among provincial cities, where the *belles - lettres* and mutual admiration were assiduously cultivated. Southey saw Norwich
at its best. Among its "superior people" were several
who really deserved something better than that vague distinction. Chief among them was Dr. Sayers, whom the
German critics compared to Gray, who had handled the
Norse mythology in poetry, who created the English mon-
odrame, and introduced the rhymeless measures followed

5

by Southey. He rested too soon upon his well-earned reputation, contented himself with touching and retouching his verses; and possessing singularly pleasing manners, abounding information and genial wit, embellished and enjoyed society.[1] William Taylor, the biographer of Sayers, was a few years his junior. He was versed in Goethe, in Schiller, in the great Kotzebue—Shakspeare's immediate successor, in Klopstock, in the fantastic ballad, in the new criticism, and all this at a time when German characters were as undecipherable to most Englishmen as Assyrian arrow-heads. The whirligig of time brought an odd revenge when Carlyle, thirty years later, hailed in Taylor the first example of "the natural-born English Philistine." In Norwich he was known as a model of filial virtue, a rising light of that illuminated city, a man whose extraordinary range pointed him out as the fit and proper person to be interrogated by any blue-stocking lady upon topics as remote as the domestic arrangements of the Chinese Emperor, Chim-Cham-Chow. William Taylor had a command of new and mysterious words: he shone in paradox, and would make ladies aghast by "defences of suicide, avowals that snuff alone had rescued him from it; information, given as certain, that 'God save the King' was sung by Jeremiah in the Temple of Solomon;"[2] with other blasphemies borrowed from the German, and too startling even for rationalistic Norwich. Dr. Enfield, from whose *Speaker* our fathers learnt to recite "My name is Norval," was no longer living; he had just departed in the odour of dilettantism. But solemn Dr. Alderson was here, and was now engaged in giving away his daughter Amelia to a divorced

[1] See Southey's article on "Dr. Sayers's Works," *Quarterly Review*, January, 1827.

[2] Harriet Martineau: Autobiography, i. p. 300.

bridegroom, the painter Opie. Just now Elizabeth Gurney was listening in the Friends' Meeting-House to that discourse which transformed her from a gay haunter of country ball-rooms to the sister and servant of Newgate prisoners. The Martineaus also were of Norwich, and upon subsequent visits the author of *Thalaba* and *Kehama* was scrutinized by the keen eyes of a little girl—not born at the date of his first visit—who smiled somewhat too early and somewhat too maliciously at the airs and affectations of her native town, and whose pleasure in pricking a windbag, literary, political, or religious, was only over-exquisite. But Harriet Martineau, who honoured courage, purity, faithfulness, and strength wherever they were found, reverenced the Tory Churchman, Robert Southey.[1]

Soon after his return from Norwich, a small house was taken at Westbury (1797), a village two miles distant from Bristol. During twelve happy months this continued to be Southey's home. "I never before or since," he says in one of the prefaces to his collected poems, "produced so much poetry in the same space of time." William Taylor, by talks about Voss and the German idylls, had set Southey thinking of a series of English Eclogues; Taylor also expressed his wonder that some one of our poets had not undertaken what the French and Germans so long supported—an Almanack of the Muses, or Annual Anthology of minor poems by various writers. The suggestion was well received by Southey, who became editor of such annual volumes for the years 1799 and 1800. At this period were produced many of the ballads and short pieces which are perhaps more generally known than any other of Southey's writings. He had served his apprenticeship to

---

[1] See her "History of the Peace," B. vi. chap. xvi.

the craft and mystery of such verse-making in the *Morning Post*, earning thereby a guinea a week, but it was not until *Bishop Bruno* was written at Westbury that he had the luck to hit off the right tone, as he conceived it, of the modern ballad.   The popularity of his *Mary the Maid of the Inn*, which unhappy children got by heart, and which some one even dramatized, was an affliction to its author, for he would rather have been remembered as a ballad writer in connexion with *Rudiger* and *Lord William*. What he has written in this kind certainly does not move the heart as with a trumpet; it does not bring with it the dim burden of sorrow which is laid upon the spirit by songs like those of Yarrow crooning of "old, unhappy, far-off things."   But to tell a tale of fantasy briefly, clearly, brightly, and at the same time with a certain heightening of imaginative touches, is no common achievement.   The spectre of the murdered boy in *Lord William* shone upon by a sudden moonbeam, and surrounded by the welter of waves, is more than a picturesque apparition; readers of goodwill may find him a very genuine little ghost, a stern and sad justicer.   What has been named "the lyrical cry" is hard to find in any of Southey's shorter poems.   In *Roderick* and elsewhere he takes delight in representing great moments of life when fates are decided; but such moments are usually represented as eminences on which will and passion wrestle in a mortal embrace, and if the cry of passion be heard, it is often a half-stifled death cry. The best of Southey's shorter poems, expressing personal feelings, are those which sum up the virtue spread over seasons of life and long habitual moods.   Sometimes he is simply sportive, as a serious man released from thought and toil may be, and at such times the sportiveness, while genuine as a schoolboy's, is, like a schoolboy's, the reverse of keen - edged; on other occasions he expresses simply a strong man's endurance of sorrow; but more often an undertone of gravity appears through his glee, and in his sorrow there is something of solemn joy.

All this year (1799) *Madoc* was steadily advancing, and *The Destruction of the Dom Daniel* had been already sketched in outline. Southey was fortunate in finding an admirable listener. The Pneumatic Institution, established in Bristol by Dr. Beddoes, was now under the care of a youth lately an apothecary's apprentice at Penzance, a poet, but still more a philosopher, "a miraculous young man." "He is not yet twenty-one, nor has he applied to chemistry more than eighteen months, but he has advanced with such seven-leagued strides as to overtake everybody. His name is Davy"—Humphry Davy—"the young chemist, the young everything, the man least ostentatious, of first talent that I have ever known." Southey would walk across from Westbury, an easy walk over beautiful ground, to breathe Davy's wonder-working gas, "which excites all possible mental and muscular energy, and induces almost a delirium of pleasurable sensations without any subsequent dejection." Pleased to find scientific proof that he possessed a poet's fine susceptibility, he records that the nitrous oxide wrought upon him more readily than upon any other of its votaries. "Oh, Tom!" he exclaims, gasping and ebullient—"oh, Tom! such a gas has Davy discovered, the gaseous oxyde! . . . Davy has actually invented a new pleasure for which language has no name. I am going for more this evening; it makes one strong, and so happy! so gloriously happy! . . . Oh, excellent air-bag!" If Southey drew inspiration from Davy's air-bag, could Davy do less than lend his ear to Southey's epic? They would stroll back to Martin Hall—so christened because the birds who

love delicate air built under its eaves their "pendant beds"
—and in the large sitting-room, its recesses stored with
books, or seated near the currant-bushes in the garden,
the tenant of Martin Hall would read aloud of Urien and
Madoc and Cadwallon. When Davy had said good-bye,
Southey would sit long in the window open to the west,
poring on the fading glories of sunset, while about him
the dew was cool, and the swallows' tiny shrieks of glee
grew less frequent, until all was hushed and another day
was done. And sometimes he would muse how all things
that he needed for utter happiness were here—all things
—and then would rise an ardent desire—except a child.

Martin Hall was unhappily held on no long lease; its
owner now required possession, and the Southeys, with
their household gods, had reluctantly to bid it farewell.
Another trouble, and a more formidable one, at the same
time threatened. What with Annual Anthologies, Madoc
in Wales, Madoc in Aztlan, the design for a great poem
on the Deluge, for a Greek drama, for a Portuguese tragedy, for a martyrdom play of the reign of Queen Mary—
what with reading Spanish, learning Dutch, translating and
reviewing for the booksellers—Southey had been too closely at work. His heart began to take fits of sudden and
violent pulsation; his sleep, ordinarily as sound as a child's,
became broken and unrefreshing. Unless the disease were
thrown off by regular exercise, Beddoes assured him, it
would fasten upon him, and could not be overcome. Two
years previously they had spent a summer at Burton, in
Hampshire; why should they not go there again? In
June, 1799, unaccompanied by his wife, whose health seemed also to be impaired, Southey went to seek a house.
Two cottages, convertible into one, with a garden, a fish-
pond, and a pigeon-house, promised a term of quiet and

comfort in "Southey Palace that is to be." Possession
was not to be had until Michaelmas, and part of the in-
tervening time was very enjoyably spent in roaming among
the vales and woods, the coombes and cliffs of Devon. It
was in some measure a renewal of the open-air delight
which had been his at the Arrabida and Cintra. "I have
seen the Valley of Stones," he writes: "Imagine a narrow
vale between two ridges of hills somewhat steep; the
southern hill turfed; the vale which runs from east to
west covered with huge stones and fragments of stones
among the fern that fills it; the northern ridge completely
bare, excoriated of all turf and all soil, the very bones and
skeleton of the earth; rock reclining upon rock, stone
piled upon stone, a huge and terrific mass. A palace of
the Preadamite kings, a city of the Anakim, must have
appeared so shapeless and yet so like the ruins of what
had been shaped, after the waters of the flood subsided.
I ascended with some toil the highest point; two large
stones inclining on each other formed a rude portal on the
summit: here I sat down; a little level platform about
two yards long lay before me, and then the eye fell im-
mediately upon the sea, far, very far below. I never felt
the sublimity of solitude before."

But Southey could not rest. "I had rather leave off
eating than poetizing," he had said; and now the words
seemed coming true, for he still poetized, and had almost
ceased to eat. "Yesterday I finished *Madoc*, thank God!
and thoroughly to my own satisfaction; but I have resolved on one great, laborious, and radical alteration. It
was my design to identify Madoc with Mango Capac, the
legislator of Peru: in this I have totally failed; therefore
Mango Capac is to be the hero of another poem." There
is something charming in the logic of Southey's "there-

fore;" so excellent an epic hero must not go to waste; but when, on the following morning, he rose early, it was to put on paper the first hundred lines, not of Mango Capac, but of the Dom Daniel poem which we know as *Thalaba*. A *Mohammed*, to be written in hexameters, was also on the stocks; and Coleridge had promised the half of this. Southey, who remembered a certain quarto volume on Pantisocracy and other great unwritten works, including the last—a Life of Lessing, by Samuel Taylor Coleridge— knew the worth of his collaborateur's promises. However, it matters little; "the only inconvenience that his dereliction can occasion will be that I shall write the poem in fragments, and have to seam them together at last." "My Mohammed will be what I believe the Arabian was in the beginning of his career—sincere in enthusiasm; and it would puzzle a casuist to distinguish between the belief of inspiration and actual enthusiasm." A short fragment of the *Mohammed* was actually written by Coleridge, and a short fragment by Southey, which, dating from 1799, have an interest in connexion with the history of the English hexameter. Last among these many projects, Southey has made up his mind to undertake one great historical work—the History of Portugal. This was no dream-project; Mango Capac never descended from his father the Sun to appear in Southey's poem; Mohammed never emerged from the cavern where the spider had spread his net; but the work which was meant to rival Gibbon's great history was in part achieved. It is a fact more pathetic than many others which make appeal for tears, that this most ambitious and most cherished design of Southey's life, conceived at the age of twenty-six, and kept constantly in view through all his days of toil, was not yet half wrought out when, forty years later, the pen dropped

from his hand, and the worn-out brain could think no
more.

The deal shavings had hardly been cleared out of the
twin cottages at Burton, when Southey was prostrated by
a nervous fever; on recovering, he moved to Bristol, still
weak, with strange pains about the heart, and sudden
seizures of the head. An entire change of scene was ob-
viously desirable. The sound of the brook that ran beside
his uncle's door at Cintra, the scent of the lemon-groves,
the grandeur of the Arrabida, haunted his memory; there
were books and manuscripts to be found in Portugal which
were essential in the preparation of his great history of
that country. Mr. Hill invited him; his good friend Elmsley, an old schoolfellow, offered him a hundred pounds.
From every point of view it seemed right and prudent to
go. Ailing and unsettled as he was, he yet found strength
and time to put his hand to a good work before leaving
Bristol. Chatterton always interested Southey deeply;
they had this much at least in common, that both had often listened to the chimes of St. Mary Redcliffe, that both
were lovers of antiquity, both were rich in store of verse,
and lacked all other riches. Chatterton's sister, Mrs. New-
ton, and her child were needy and neglected. It occurred
to Southey and Cottle that an edition of her brother's
poems might be published for her benefit. Subscribers
came in slowly, and the plan underwent some alterations;
but in the end the charitable thought bore fruit, and the
sister and niece of the great unhappy boy were lifted into
security and comfort. To have done something to appease
the moody and indignant spirit of a dead poet, was well;
to have rescued from want a poor woman and her daughter,
was perhaps even better.

Early in April, 1800, Southey was once more on his way

4

from Bristol, by Falmouth, to the Continent, accompanied
by his wife, now about to be welcomed to Portugal by the
fatherly uncle whose prudence she had once alarmed. The
wind was adverse, and while the travellers were detained
Southey strolled along the beach, caught soldier-crabs, and
observed those sea-anemones which blossom anew in the
verse of Thalaba. For reading on the voyage, he had
brought Burns, Coleridge's poems, the Lyrical Ballads, and
a poem, with "miraculous beauties," called *Gebir*, "written
by God knows who." But when the ship lost sight of England, Southey, with swimming head, had little spirit left for
wrestling with the intractable thews of Landor's early verse;
he could just grunt out some crooked pun or quaint phrase
in answer to inquiries as to how he did. Suddenly, on
the fourth morning, came the announcement that a French
cutter was bearing down upon them. Southey leaped to
his feet, hurriedly removed his wife to a place of safety,
and, musket in hand, took his post upon the quarter-deck.
The smoke from the enemy's matches could be seen. She
was hailed, answered in broken English, and passed on. A
moment more, and the suspense was over; she was English,
manned from Guernsey. "You will easily imagine," says
Southey, "that my sensations at the ending of the business
were very definable—one honest, simple joy that I was in
a whole skin!" Two mornings more, and the sun rose behind the Berlings; the heights of Cintra became visible,
and nearer, the silver dust of the breakers, with sea-gulls
sporting over them; a pilot's boat, with puffed and flap-
ping sail, ran out; they passed thankfully our Lady of the
Guide, and soon dropped anchor in the Tagus. An absence of four years had freshened every object to Southey's
sense of seeing, and now he had the joy of viewing all familiar things as strange through so dear a companion's eyes.

Mr. Hill was presently on board with kindly greeting; he had hired a tiny house for them, perched well above the river, its little rooms cool with many doors and windows. Manuel the barber, brisk as Figaro, would be their factotum, and Mrs. Southey could also see a new maid—Maria Rosa. Maria by-and-by came to be looked at, in powder, straw-coloured gloves, fan, pink-ribands, muslin petticoat, green satin sleeves; she was "not one of the folk who sleep on straw mattresses;" withal she was young and clean. Mrs. Southey, who had liked little the prospect of being thrown abroad upon the world, was beginning to be reconciled to Portugal; roses and oranges and green peas in early May were pleasant things. Then the streets were an unending spectacle; now a negro going by with Christ in a glass case, to be kissed for a petty alms; now some picturesque, venerable beggar; now the little Emperor of the Holy Ghost, strutting it from Easter till Whitsuntide, a six-year-old mannikin with silk stockings, buckles, cocked hat, and sword, his gentlemen ushers attending, and his servants receiving donations on silver salvers. News of an assassination, from time to time, did not much disturb the tranquil tenor of ordinary life. There were old gardens to loiter in along vine-trellised walks, or in sunshine where the grey lizards glanced and gleamed. And eastward from the city were lovely by-lanes amid blossoming olive-trees or market-gardens, veined by tiny aqueducts and musical with the creak of water-wheels, which told of cool refreshment. There was also the vast public aqueduct to visit; Edith Southey, holding her husband's hand, looked down, hardly discovering the diminished figures below of women washing in the brook of Alcantara. If the sultry noon in Lisbon was hard to endure, evening made amends; then strong sea-winds swept the narrowest alley, and rolled their current down every avenue. And later, it was pure content to look down upon the moonlighted river, with Almada stretching its black isthmus into the waters that shone like midnight snow.

Before moving to Cintra, they wished to witness the procession of the Body of God—Southey likes the English words as exposing "the naked nonsense of the blasphemy"—those of St. Anthony, and the Heart of Jesus, and the first bull-fight. Everything had grown into one insufferable glare; the very dust was bleached; the light was like the quivering of a furnace fire. Every man and beast was asleep; the stone-cutter slept with his head upon the stone; the dog slept under the very cart-wheels; the bells alone slept not, nor ceased from their importunate clamour. At length—it was near mid-June—a marvellous cleaning of streets took place, the houses were hung with crimson damask, soldiers came and lined the ways, windows and balconies filled with impatient watchers—not a jewel in Lisbon but was on show. With blare of music the procession began; first, the banners of the city and its trades, the clumsy bearers crab-sidling along; an armed champion carrying a flag; wooden St. George held painfully on horseback; led horses, their saddles covered with rich escutcheons; all the brotherhoods, an immense train of men in red or grey cloaks; the knights of the orders superbly dressed; the whole patriarchal church in glorious robes; and then, amid a shower of rose-leaves fluttering from the windows, the Pix, and after the Pix, the Prince. On a broiling Sunday, the amusement being cool and devout, was celebrated the bull-feast. The first wound sickened Edith; Southey himself, not without an effort, looked on and saw "the death-sweat darkening the dun hide"—a circumstance borne in mind for his *Thalaba*. "I am not quite sure," he writes, "that my curiosity in once going was perfectly justifiable, but the pain inflicted by the sight was expiation enough."

After this it was high time to take refuge from the sun among the lemon-groves at Cintra. Here, if ever in his life, Southey for a brief season believed that the grasshopper is wiser than the ant; a true Portuguese indolence overpowered him. "I have spent my mornings half naked in a wet room dozing upon the bed, my right hand not daring to touch my left." Such glorious indolence could only be a brief possession with Southey. More often he would wander by the streams to those spots where purple crocuses carpeted the ground, and there rest and read. Sometimes seated sideways on one of the surefooted *burros*, with a boy to beat and guide the brute, he would jog lazily on, while Edith, now skilled in "ass-womanship," would jog along on a brother donkey. Once and again a fog—not unwelcome—came rolling in from the ocean, one huge mass of mist, marching through the valley like a victorious army, approaching, blotting the brightness, but leaving all dank and fresh. And always the evenings were delightful, when fireflies sparkled under the trees, or in July and August, as their light went out, when the grillo began his song. "I eat oranges, figs, and delicious pears —drink Colares wine, a sort of half-way excellence between port and claret—read all I can lay my hands on—dream of poem after poem, and play after play—take a siesta of two hours, and am as happy as if life were but one everlasting to-day, and that to-morrow was not to be provided for."

But Southey's second visit to Portugal was, on the whole, no season of repose. A week in the southern climate seemed to have restored him to health, and he assailed folio after folio in his uncle's library, rising each morning at five, "to lay in bricks for the great Pyramid of my history." The chronicles, the laws, the poetry of Portugal, were among these bricks. Nor did he slacken in his ardour as a writer of verse. Six books of *Thalaba* were in his trunk in manuscript when he sailed from Falmouth; the remaining six were of a southern birth. "I am busy," he says, "in correcting *Thalaba* for the press. . . . It is a good job done, and so I have thought of another, and another, and another." As with *Joan of Arc*, so with this maturer poem the correction was a rehandling which doubled the writer's work. To draw the pen across six hundred lines did not cost him a pang. At length the manuscript was despatched to his friend Rickman, with instructions to make as good a bargain as he could for the first thousand copies. By *Joan* and the miscellaneous *Poems* of 1797, Southey had gained not far from a hundred and fifty pounds; he might fairly expect a hundred guineas for *Thalaba*. It would buy the furniture of his long-expected house. But he was concerned about the prospects of Harry, his younger brother; and now William Taylor wrote that some provincial surgeon of eminence would board and instruct the lad during four or five years for precisely a hundred guineas. "A hundred guineas!" Southey exclaims; "well, but, thank God, there is *Thalaba* ready, for which I ask this sum." "*Thalaba* finished, all my poetry," he writes, "instead of being wasted in rivulets and ditches, shall flow into the great Madoc Mississippi river." One epic poem, however, he finds too little to content him; already *The Curse of Kehama* is in his head, and another of the mythological series which never saw the light. "I have some distant view of manufacturing a Hindoo romance. wild as *Thalaba:* and a nearer one of a

Persian story, of which I see the germ of vitality. I take the system of the Zendavesta for my mythology, and introduce the powers of darkness persecuting a Persian, one of the hundred and fifty sons of the great king; an Athenian captive is a prominent character, and the whole warfare of the evil power ends in exalting a Persian prince into a citizen of Athens." From which catastrophe we may infer that Southey had still something republican about his heart.

Before quitting Portugal, the Southeys, with their friend Waterhouse and a party of ladies, travelled northwards, encountering very gallantly the trials of the way; Mafra, its convent and library, had been already visited by Southey. "Do you love reading?" asked the friar who accompanied them, overhearing some remark about the books. "Yes." "And I," said the honest Franciscan, "love eating and drinking." At Coimbra—that central point from which radiates the history and literature of Portugal — Southey would have agreed feelingly with the good brother of the Mafra convent; he had looked forward to precious moments of emotion in that venerable city; but air and exercise had given him a cruel appetite; if truth must be told, the ducks of the monastic poultry-yard were more to him than the precious finger of St. Anthony. "I *did* long," he confesses, "to buy, beg, or steal a dinner." The dinner must somehow have been secured before he could approach in a worthy spirit that most affecting monument at Coimbra — the Fountain of Tears. "It is the spot where Inez de Castro was accustomed to meet her husband Pedro, and weep for him in his absence. Certainly her dwelling-house was in the adjoining garden; and from there she was dragged, to be murdered at the feet of the king, her father-in-law.... I, who have long

planned a tragedy upon the subject, stood upon my own
scene." While Southey and his companions gazed at
the fountains and their shadowing cedar-trees, the gowns-
men gathered round; the visitors were travel-stained and
bronzed by the sun; perhaps the witty youths cheered
for the lady with the squaw tint; whatever offence may
have been given, the ladies' protectors found them "impu-
dent blackguards," and with difficulty suppressed pugilistic
risings.

After an excursion southwards to Algarve, Southey
made ready for his return to England (1801). His wife
desired it, and he had attained the main objects of his
sojourn abroad. His health had never been more perfect;
he had read widely; he had gathered large material for
his History; he knew where to put his hand on this or
that which might prove needful, whenever he should return to complete his work among the libraries of Portugal.
On arriving at Bristol, a letter from Coleridge met him.
It was dated from Greta Hall, Keswick; and after remind-
ing Southey that Bristol had recently lost the miraculous
young man, Davy, and adding that he, Samuel Taylor Coleridge, had experiences, sufferings, hopes, projects to im-
part, which would beguile much time, "were you on a
desert island and I your *Friday*," it went on to present
the attractions of Keswick, and in particular of Greta Hall,
in a way which could not be resisted. Taking all in all—
the beauty of the prospect, the roominess of the house,
the lowness of the rent, the unparalleled merits of the
landlord, the neighbourhood of noble libraries—it united
advantages not to be found together elsewhere. "In
short"—the appeal wound up—"for situation and con-
venience — and when I mention the name of Wordsworth, for society of men of intellect—I know no place

in which you and Edith would find yourselves so well
suited."

Meanwhile Drummond, an M.P. and a translator of Persius, who was going as ambassador, first to Palermo and
then to Constantinople, was on the look-out for a secretary. The post would be obtained for Southey by his
friend Wynn, if possible; this might lead to a consulship;
why not to the consulship at Lisbon, with 1000*l.* a year?
Such possibilities, however, could not prevent him from
speedily visiting Coleridge and Keswick. "Time and absence make strange work with our affections," so writes
Southey; "but mine are ever returning to rest upon you.
I have other and dear friends, but none with whom the
whole of my being is intimate. . . . Oh! I have yet such
dreams. Is it quite clear that you and I were not meant
for some better star, and dropped by mistake into this
world of pounds, shillings, and pence?" So for the first
time Southey set foot in Keswick, and looked upon the
lake and the hills which were to become a portion of his
being, and which have taken him so closely, so tenderly, to
themselves. His first feeling was one not precisely of disappointment, but certainly of remoteness from this northern landscape; he had not yet come out from the glow
and the noble *abandon* of the South. "These lakes," he
says, "are like rivers; but oh for the Mondego and the
Tagus! And these mountains, beautifully indeed are they
shaped and grouped; but oh for the grand Monchique!
and for Cintra, my paradise!"

Time alone was needed to calm and temper his sense of
seeing; for when, leaving Mrs. Southey with her sister and
Coleridge, he visited his friend Wynn at Llangedwin, and
breathed the mountain air of his own Prince Madoc, all
the loveliness of Welsh streams and rivers sank into his

6

soul. "The Dee is broad and shallow, and its dark waters shiver into white and silver and hues of amber brown.
No mud upon the shore—no bushes—no marsh plants—
anywhere a child might stand dry-footed and dip his hand
into the water." And again a contrasted picture: "The
mountain-side was stony, and a few trees grew among its
stones; the other side was more wooded, and had grass on
the top, and a huge waterfall thundered into the bottom,
and thundered down the bottom. When it had nearly
passed these rocky straits, it met another stream. The
width of water then became considerable, and twice it
formed a large black pool, to the eye absolutely stagnant,
the froth of the waters that entered there sleeping upon
the surface; it had the deadness of enchantment; yet was
not the pool wider than the river above it and below it,
where it foamed over and fell." Such free delight as
Southey had among the hills of Wales came quickly to an
end. A letter was received offering him the position of
private secretary to Mr. Corry, Chancellor of the Excheq-
uer for Ireland, with a salary of four hundred pounds a
year. Rickman was in Dublin, and this was Rickman's
doing. Southey, as he was in prudence bound to do, accepted the appointment, hastened back to Keswick, bade
farewell for a little while to his wife, and started for Dublin in no cheerful frame of mind.

At a later time, Southey possessed Irish friends whom
he honoured and loved; he has written wise and humane
words about the Irish people. But all through his career
Ireland was to Southey somewhat too much that ideal
country—of late to be found only in the region of humor-
ous-pathetic melodrama—in which the business of life is
carried on mainly by the agency of bulls and blunder-
busses; and it required a distinct effort on his part to con-

ceive the average Teague or Patrick otherwise than as a
potato-devouring troglodyte, on occasions grotesquely amiable, but more often with the rage of Popery working in
his misproportioned features.   Those hours during which
Southey waited for the packet were among the heaviest
of his existence.   After weary tackings in a baffling wind,
the ship was caught into a gale, and was whirled away,
fifteen miles north of Dublin, to the fishing-town of
Balbriggan.   Then, a drive across desolate country, which
would have depressed the spirits had it not been enlivened
by the airs and humours of little Dr. Solomon, the unique,
the omniscient, the garrulous, next after Bonaparte the
most illustrious of mortals, inventor of the Cordial Balm
of Gilead, and possessor of a hundred puncheons of rum.
When the new private secretary arrived, the chancellor
was absent; the secretary, therefore, set to work on re-
building a portion of his *Madoc*.   Presently Mr. Corry
appeared, and there was a bow and a shake of hands;
then he hurried away to London, to be followed by
Southey, who, going round by Keswick, was there joined
by his wife.   From London Southey writes to Rickman,
"The chancellor and the scribe go on in the same way.
The scribe hath made out a catalogue of all books published since the commencement of '97 upon finance and
scarcity; he hath also copied a paper written by J. R.
[John Rickman] containing some Irish alderman's hints
about oak-bark; and nothing more hath the scribe done
in his vocation.   Duly he calls at the chancellor's door;
sometimes he is admitted to immediate audience; sometimes kicketh his heels in the antechamber; . . . sometimes a gracious message emancipates him for the day.
Secrecy hath been enjoined him as to these State proceed-
ings.   On three subjects he is directed to read and re-

search—corn-laws, finance, tythes, according to their written order." The independent journals meanwhile had
compared Corry and Southey, the two State conspirators,
to Empson and Dudley; and delicately expressed a hope
that the poet would make no false *numbers* in his new work.

Southey, who had already worn an ass's head in one of
Gillray's caricatures, was not afflicted by the newspaper
sarcasm; but the vacuity of such a life was intolerable;
and when it was proposed that he should become tutor to
Corry's son, he brought his mind finally to the point of
resigning "a foolish office and a good salary." His notions of competence were moderate; the vagabondage between the Irish and English headquarters entailed by his
office was irksome. His books were accumulating, and
there was ample work to be done among them if he had
but a quiet library of his own. Then, too, there was another good reason for resigning. A new future was opening
for Southey. Early in the year (1802) his mother died.
She had come to London to be with her son; there she
had been stricken with mortal illness; true to her happy,
self-forgetful instincts, she remained calm, uncomplaining,
considerate for others. "Go down, my dear; I shall sleep
presently," she had said, knowing that death was at hand.
With his mother, the last friend of Southey's infancy and
childhood was gone. "I calmed and curbed myself," he
writes, "and forced myself to employment; but at night
there was no sound of feet in her bedroom, to which I
had been used to listen, and in the morning it was not my
first business to see her." The past was past indeed. But
as the year opened, it brought a happy promise; before
summer would end, a child might be in his arms. Here
were sufficient reasons for his resignation; a library and a
nursery ought, he says, to be stationary.

To Bristol husband and wife came, and there found a small furnished house.   After the roar of Fleet Street, and the gathering of distinguished men—Fuseli, Flaxman, Barry, Lamb, Campbell, Bowles—there was a strangeness in the great quiet of the place.   But in that quiet Southey could observe each day the growth of the pile of manuscript containing his version of *Amadis of Gaul*, for which Longman and Rees promised him a munificent sixty pounds. He toiled at his *History of Portugal*, finding matter of special interest in that part which was concerned with the religious orders.   He received from his Lisbon collection precious boxes folio-crammed.   "My dear and noble books !   Such folios of saints ! dull books enough for my patience to diet upon, till all my flock be gathered together into one fold."   Sixteen volumes of Spanish poetry are lying uncut in the next room ; a folio yet untasted jogs his elbow ; two of the best and rarest chronicles coyly invite him.   He had books enough in England to employ three years of active industry.   And underlying all thoughts of the great Constable Nuño Alvares Pereyra, of the King D. João I., and of the Cid, deeper than the sportsman pleasure of hunting from their lair strange facts about the orders Cistercian, Franciscan, Dominican, Jesuit, there was a thought of that new-comer whom, says Southey, "I already feel disposed to call whelp and dog, and all those vocables of vituperation by which a man loves to call those he loves best."

In September, 1802, was born Southey's first child, named Margaret Edith, after her mother and her dead grandmother ; a flat-nosed, round-foreheaded, grey-eyed, good-humoured girl.   "I call Margaret," he says, in a sober mood of fatherly happiness, "by way of avoiding all commonplace phraseology of endearment, a worthy child and

a most excellent character. She loves me better than any
one except her mother; her eyes are as quick as thought;
she is all life and spirit, and as happy as the day is long;
but that little brain of hers is never at rest, and it is painful to see how dreams disturb her." For Margery and
her mother and the folios a habitation must be found.
Southey inclined now towards settling in the neighbourhood of London—now towards Norwich, where Dr. Sayers
and William Taylor would welcome him — now towards
Keswick; but its horrid latitude, its incessant rains! On
the whole, his heart turned most fondly to Wales; and
there, in one of the loveliest spots of Great Britain, in the
Vale of Neath, was a house to let, by name Maes Gwyn.
Southey gave his fancy the rein, and pictured himself
"housed and homed" in Maes Gwyn, working steadily at
the *History of Portugal*, and now and again glancing away
from his work to have a look at Margery seated in her
little great chair. But it was never to be; a difference
with the landlord brought to an end his treaty for the
house, and in August the child lay dying. It was bitter
to part with what had been so long desired—during sev-
en childless years — and what had grown so dear. But
Southey's heart was strong; he drew himself together, returned to his toil, now less joyous than before, and set
himself to strengthen and console his wife.

Bristol was henceforth a place of mournful memories.
"Edith," writes Southey, "will be nowhere so well as
with her sister Coleridge. She has a little girl some six
months old, and I shall try and graft her into the wound
while it is yet fresh." Thus Greta Hall received its guests
(September, 1803). At first the sight of little Sara Coleridge and her baby cooings caused shootings of pain on
which Southey had not counted. Was the experiment of

this removal to prove a failure? He still felt as if he were a feather driven by the wind. "I have no symptoms of root-striking here," he said. But he spoke, not knowing what was before him; the years of wandering were indeed over; here he had found his home.

CHAPTER IV.

WAYS OF LIFE AT KESWICK, 1803—1839.

THE best of life with Southey was yet to come; but in what remains there are few outstanding events to chronicle; there is nowhere any splendour of circumstance. Of some lives the virtue is distilled, as it were, into a few exquisite moments—moments of rapture, of vision, of sudden and shining achievement; all the days and years seem to exist only for the sake of such faultless moments, and it matters little whether such a life, of whose very essence it is to break the bounds of time and space, be long or short as measured by the falling of sandgrains or the creeping of a shadow. Southey's life was not one of these; its excellence was constant, uniform, perhaps somewhat too evenly distributed. He wrought in his place day after day, season after season. He submitted to the good laws of use and wont. He grew stronger, calmer, more full-fraught with stores of knowledge, richer in treasure of the heart. Time laid its hand upon him gently and unfalteringly: the bounding step became less light and swift; the ringing voice lapsed into sadder fits of silence; the raven hair changed to a snowy white; only still the indefatigable eye ran down the long folio columns, and the indefatigable hand still held the pen—until all true life had ceased. When it has been said that Southey was appointed Pye's successor in the laureateship, that he received an honorary degree from his university, that now and again he visited the Continent, that children were born to him from among whom death made choice of the dearest; and when we add that he wrote and published books, the leading facts of Southey's life have been told. Had he been a worse or a weaker man, we might look to find mysteries, picturesque vices, or engaging follies; as it is, everything is plain, straightforward, substantial. What makes the life of Southey eminent and singular is its unity of purpose, its persistent devotion to a chosen object, its simplicity, purity, loyalty, fortitude, kindliness, truth.

The river Greta, before passing under the bridge at the end of Main Street, Keswick, winds about the little hill on which stands Greta Hall; its murmur may be heard when all is still beyond the garden and orchard; to the west it catches the evening light. "In front," Coleridge wrote when first inviting his friend to settle with him, "we have a giants' camp—an encamped army of tent-like mountains, which by an inverted arch gives a view of another vale. On our right the lovely vale and the wedge-shaped lake of Bassenthwaite; and on our left Derwentwater and Lodore full in view, and the fantastic mountains of Borrowdale. Behind us the massy Skiddaw, smooth, green, high, with two chasms and a tent-like ridge in the larger." Southey's house belongs in a peculiar degree to his life: in it were stored the treasures upon which his intellect drew for sustenance; in it his affections found their earthly abiding-place; all the most mirthful, all the most mournful, recollections of Southey hang about it; to it in every little wandering his heart reverted like an exile's; it was at once his workshop and his playground; and for a time, while he endured a living death, it became his antechamber to the tomb. The rambling tenement consisted of two houses under one roof, the larger part being occupied by the Coleridges and Southeys, the smaller for a time by Mr. Jackson, their landlord. On the ground-floor was the parlour which served as dining-room and general sitting-room, a pleasant chamber looking upon the green in front; here also were Aunt Lovell's sitting-room, and the mangling-room, in which stood ranged in a row the long array of clogs, from the greatest even unto the least, figuring in a symbol the various stages of human life. The stairs to the right of the kitchen led to a landing-place filled with bookcases; a few steps more led to the little bedroom occupied by Mrs. Coleridge and her daughter. "A few steps farther," writes Sara Coleridge, whose description is here given in abridgment, " was a little wing bedroom—then the study, where my uncle sat all day occupied with literary labours and researches, but which was used as a drawing-room for company. Here all the tea-visiting guests were received. The room had three windows, a large one looking down upon the green with the wide flower-border, and over to Keswick Lake and mountains beyond. There were two smaller windows looking towards the lower part of the town seen beyond the nursery-garden. The room was lined with books in fine bindings; there were books also in brackets, elegantly lettered vellum-covered volumes lying on their sides in a heap. The walls were hung with pictures, mostly portraits. . . . At the back of the room was a comfortable sofa, and there were sundry tables, beside my uncle's library table, his screen, desk, etc. Altogether, with its internal fittings up, its noble outlook, and something pleasing in its proportions, this was a charming room." Hard by the study was Southey's bedroom. We need not ramble farther through passages lined with books, and up and down flights of stairs to Mr. Jackson's organ-room, and Mrs. Lovell's room, and Hartley's parlour, and the nurseries, and the dark apple-room supposed to be the abode of a bogle. Without, greensward, flowers, shrubs, strawberry-beds, fruit-trees, encircled the house; to the back, beyond the orchard, a little wood stretched down to the river-side. A rough path ran along the bottom of the wood; here, on a covered seat, Southey often read or planned future work, and here his little niece loved to play in sight of the dimpling water. "Dear Greta Hall!" she exclaims; "and oh, that rough path beside the Greta! How much of my childhood, of my girlhood, of my youth, were spent there!"

Southey's attachment to his mountain town and its lakes was of no sudden growth. He came to them as one not born under their influence; that power of hills to which Wordsworth owed fealty, had not brooded upon Southey during boyhood; the rich southern meadows, the wooded cliffs of Avon, the breezy downs, had nurtured his imagination, and to these he was still bound by pieties of the heart. In the churchyard at Ashton, where lay his father and his kinsfolk, the beneficent cloud of mingled love and sorrow most overshadowed his spirit. His imagination did not soar, as did Wordsworth's, in naked solitudes; he did not commune with a Presence immanent in external nature: the world, as he viewed it, was an admirable habitation for mankind—a habitation with a history. Even after he had grown a mountaineer, he loved a humanized landscape, one in which the gains of man's courage, toil, and endurance are apparent. Flanders, where the spade has wrought its miracles of diligence, where the slow canal-boat glides, where the *carillons* ripple from old spires, where sturdy burghers fought for freedom, and where vellum-bound quartos might be sought and found, Flanders, on the whole, gave Southey deeper and stronger feelings than did Switzerland. The ideal land of his dreams was always Spain; the earthly paradise for him was Cintra, with its glory of sun, and a glow even in its depths of shadow. But as the years went by, Spain became more and more a memory, less and less a hope; and the realities of life in his home were of more worth every day. When, in 1807, it grew clear that Greta Hall was to be his life-long place of abode, Southey's heart closed upon it with a tenacious grasp. He set the plasterer and carpenter to work; he planted shrubs; he enclosed the garden; he gathered his books about him, and thought that here were materials for the industry of many years; he held in his arms children who were born in this new home; and he looked to Crosthwaite Churchyard, expecting, with quiet satisfaction, that when toil was ended he should there take his rest.

"I don't talk much about these things," Southey writes; "but these lakes and mountains give me a deep joy for which I suspect nothing elsewhere can compensate, and this is a feeling which time strengthens instead of weakening." Some of the delights of southern counties he missed; his earliest and deepest recollections were connected with flowers; both flowers and fruits were now too few; there was not a cowslip to be found near Keswick. "Here in Cumberland I miss the nightingale and the violet—the most delightful bird and the sweetest flower." But for such losses there were compensations. A pastoral land will give amiable pledges for the seasons and the months, and will perform its engagements with a punctual observance; to this the mountains hardly condescend, but they shower at their will a sudden largess of unimagined beauty. Southey would sally out for a constitutional at his

three-mile pace, the peaked cap slightly shadowing his
eyes, which were coursing over the pages of a book held
open as he walked; he had left his study to obtain exercise, and so to preserve health; he was not a laker engaged
in view-hunting; he did not affect the contemplative mood
which at the time was not and could not be his. But when
he raised his eyes, or when, quickening his three-mile to a
four-mile pace, he closed the book, the beauty which lay
around him liberated and soothed his spirit. This it did
unfailingly; and it might do more, for incalculable splen-
dours, visionary glories, exaltations, terrors, are momentari-
ly possible where mountain, and cloud, and wind, and sunshine meet. Southey, as he says, did not talk much of
these things, but they made life for him immeasurably
better than it would have been in city confinement; there
were spaces, vistas, an atmosphere around his sphere of
work, which lightened and relieved it. The engagements
in his study were always so numerous and so full of interest that it needed an effort to leave the table piled with
books and papers. But a May morning would draw him
forth into the sun in spite of himself. Once abroad,
Southey had a vigorous joy in the quickened blood, and
the muscles impatient with energy long pent up. The
streams were his especial delight; he never tired of their
deep retirement, their shy loveliness, and their melody;
they could often beguile him into an hour of idle meditation; their beauty has in an especial degree passed into
his verse. When his sailor brother Thomas came and settled in the Vale of Newlands, Southey would quickly cover the ground from Keswick at his four-mile pace, and in
the beck at the bottom of Tom's fields, on summer days,
he would plunge and re-plunge and act the river-god in
the natural seats of mossy stone. Or he would be over-

powered some autumn morning by the clamour of childish
voices voting a holiday by acclamation. Their father must
accompany them; it would do him good, they knew it
would; they knew he did not take sufficient exercise, for
they had heard him say so. Where should the scramble
be? To Skiddaw Dod, or Causey Pike, or Watenlath, or,
as a compromise between their exuberant activity and his
inclination for the chair and the fireside, to Walla Crag?
And there, while his young companions opened their bas-
kets and took their noonday meal, Southey would seat
himself—as Westall has drawn him—upon the bough of
an ash-tree, the water flowing smooth and green at his
feet, but a little higher up broken, flashing, and whitening
in its fall; and there in the still autumn noon he would
muse happily, placidly, not now remembering with over-
keen desire the gurgling tanks and fountains of Cintra, his
Paradise of early manhood.[1]

On summer days, when the visits of friends, or strangers
bearing letters of introduction, compelled him to idleness,
Southey's more ambitious excursions were taken. But he
was well aware that those who form acquaintance with a
mountain region during a summer all blue and gold, know
little of its finer power. It is October that brings most
often those days faultless, pearl-pure, of affecting influence,

> "In the long year set
> Like captain jewels in the carcanet."

Then, as Wordsworth has said, the atmosphere seems refined, and the sky rendered more crystalline, as the vivify-
ing heat of the year abates; the lights and shadows are
more delicate; the colouring is richer and more finely

[1] For Westall's drawing, and the description of Walla Crag, see
"Sir Thomas More:" Colloquy VI.

harmonized; and, in this season of stillness, the ear being unoccupied, or only gently excited, the sense of vision becomes more susceptible of its appropriate enjoyments. Even December is a better month than July for perceiving the special greatness of a mountainous country. When the snow lies on the fells soft and smooth, Grisedale Pike and Skiddaw drink in tints at morning and evening marvellous as those seen upon Mont Blanc or the Jungfrau for purity and richness.

"Summer," writes Southey, "is not the season for this country. Coleridge says, and says well, that then it is like a theatre at noon. There are no *goings on* under a clear sky; but at other seasons there is such shifting of shades, such islands of light, such columns and buttresses of sunshine, as might almost make a painter burn his brushes, as the sorcerers did their books of magic when they saw the divinity which rested upon the apostles. The very snow, which you would perhaps think must monotonize the mountains, gives new varieties; it brings out their recesses and designates all their inequalities; it impresses a better feeling of their height; and it reflects such tints of saffron, or fawn, or rose-colour to the evening sun. *O Maria Santissima!* Mount Horeb, with the glory upon its summit, might have been more glorious, but not more beautiful than old Skiddaw in his winter pelisse. I will not quarrel with frost, though the fellow has the impudence to take me by the nose. The lake-side has such ten thousand charms: a fleece of snow or of the hoar-frost lies on the fallen trees or large stones; the grass-points, that just peer above the water, are powdered with diamonds; the ice on the margin with chains of crystal, and such veins and wavy lines of beauty as mock all art; and, to crown all, Coleridge and I have found out that stones thrown upon the lake when frozen make a noise like singing birds, and when you whirl on it a large flake of ice, away the shivers slide, chirping and warbling like a flight of finches." This tells of a February at Keswick; the following describes the *goings on* under an autumn sky :—" The mountains on Thursday evening, before the sun was quite down, or the moon bright, were all of one dead-blue colour; their rifts and rocks and swells and scars had all disappeared— the surface was perfectly uniform, nothing but the outline distinct; and this even surface of dead blue, from its unnatural uniformity, made them, though not transparent, appear transvious—as though they were of some soft or cloudy texture through which you could have passed. I never saw any appearance so perfectly unreal. Sometimes a blazing sunset seems to steep them through and through with red light; or it is a cloudy morning, and the sunshine slants down through a rift in the clouds, and the pillar of light makes the spot whereon it falls so emerald green, that it looks like a little field of Paradise. At night you lose the mountains, and the wind so stirs up the lake that it looks like the sea by moonlight."

If Southey had not a companion by his side, the solitude of his ramble was unbroken; he never had the knack of forgathering with chance acquaintance. With intellectual and moral boldness, and with high spirits, he united a constitutional bashfulness and reserve. His retired life, his habits of constant study, and, in later years, his shortness of sight, fell in with this infirmity. He would not patronize his humbler neighbours; he had a kind of imaginative jealousy on behalf of their rights as independent persons; and he could not be sure of straightway discovering, by any genius or instinct of good-fellowship, that common ground whereon strangers are at home with one an-

other.   Hence—and Southey himself wished that it had
been otherwise—long as he resided at Keswick, there were
perhaps not twenty persons of the lower ranks whom he
knew by sight.   "After slightly returning the salutation
of some passer-by," says his son, "he would again mechanically lift his cap as he heard some well-known name in
reply to his inquiries, and look back with regret that the
greeting had not been more cordial."

If the ice were fairly broken, he found it natural to be
easy and familiar, and by those whom he employed he was
regarded with affectionate reverence.   Mrs. Wilson—kind
and generous creature—remained in Greta Hall tending the
children as they grew up, until she died, grieved for by the
whole household.   Joseph Glover, who created the scare-
crow "Statues" for the garden—male and female created
he them, as the reader may see them figured toward the
close of *The Doctor*—Glover, the artist who set up Edith's
fantastic chimney-piece ("Well, Miss Southey," cried honest Joseph, "I've done my Devils"), was employed by
Southey during five-and-twenty years, ever since he was a
'prentice-boy.   If any warm-hearted neighbour, known or
unknown to him, came forward with a demand on Southey's sympathies, he was sure to meet a neighbourly re-
sponse.   When the miller, who had never spoken to him
before, invited the laureate to rejoice with him over the
pig he had killed — the finest ever fattened — and when
Southey was led to the place where that which had ceased
to be pig and was not yet bacon, was hung up by the hind
feet, he filled up the measure of the good man's joy by
hearty appreciation of a porker's points.   But Cumberland enthusiasm seldom flames abroad with so prodigal a
blaze as that of the worthy miller's heart.

Within the charmed circle of home, Southey's temper

G 5   7

and manners were full of a strong and sweet hilarity; and
the home circle was in itself a considerable group of persons.   The Pantisocratic scheme of a community was,
after all, near finding a fulfilment, only that the Greta ran
by in place of the Susquehanna, and that Southey took
upon his own shoulders the work of the dead Lovell, and
of Coleridge, who lay in weakness and dejection, whelmed
under the tide of dreams.   For some little time Coleridge
continued to reside at Keswick, an admirable companion
in almost all moods of mind, for all kinds of wisdom, and
all kinds of nonsense.   When he was driven abroad in
search of health, it seemed as if a brightness were gone
out of the air, and the horizon of life had grown definite
and contracted.   "It is now almost ten years," Southey
writes, "since he and I first met in my rooms at Oxford,
which meeting decided the destiny of both. . . . I am perpetually pained at thinking what he ought to be, . . . but
the tidings of his death would come upon me more like
a stroke of lightning than any evil I have ever yet endured."

Mrs. Coleridge, with her children, remained at Greta
Hall.   That quaint little metaphysician, Hartley—now an-
swering to the name of Moses, now to that of Job, the
oddest of all God's creatures—was an unceasing wonder
and delight to his uncle : "a strange, strange boy, 'ex-
quisitely wild,' an utter visionary, like the moon among
thin clouds, he moves in a circle of his own making.   He
alone is a light of his own.   Of all human beings I never
saw one so utterly naked of self."   When his father expressed surprise that Hartley should take his pleasure of
wheel-barrow-riding so sadly, "The pity is"—explained little Job—"the pity is, *I'se* always thinking of my thoughts."
" 'I'm a boy of a very religious turn,' he says; for he always talks of himself and examines his own character, just

as if he were speaking of another person, and as impartially. Every night he makes an extempore prayer aloud; but it is always in bed, and not till he is comfortable there and got into the mood. When he is ready, he touches Mrs. Wilson, who sleeps with him, and says, ' Now listen !' and off he sets like a preacher." Younger than Hartley was Derwent Coleridge, a fair, broad-chested boy, with merry eye and roguish lips, now grown out of that yellow frock in which he had earned his name of Stumpy Canary. Sara Coleridge, when her uncle came to Keswick after the death of his own Margery, was a little grand-lama at that worshipful age of seven months. A fall into the Greta, a year and a half later, helped to change her to the delicate creature whose large blue eyes would look up timidly from under her lace border and mufflings of muslin. No feeling towards their father save a reverent loyalty did the Coleridge children ever learn under Southey's roof. But when the pale-faced wanderer returned from Italy, he surprised and froze his daughter by a sudden revelation of that jealousy which is the fond injustice of an unsatisfied heart, and which a child who has freely given and taken love finds it hard to comprehend. " I think my dear father," writes Sara Coleridge, " was anxious that I should learn to love him and the Wordsworths and their children, and not cling so exclusively to my mother and all around me at home." Love him and revere his memory she did; to Wordsworth she was conscious of owing more than to any other teacher or inspirer in matters of the intellect and imagination. But in matters of the heart and conscience the daily life of Southey was the book in which she read; he was, she would emphatically declare, " upon the whole, the best man she had ever known."

But the nepotism of the most " nepotious " uncle is

not a perfect substitute for fatherhood with its hopes and
fears.   May-morning of the year 1804 saw " an Edithling
very, very ugly, with no more beauty than a young dodo,"
nestling by Edith Southey's side.   A trembling thankfulness possessed the little one's father; but when the Arc-
tic weather changed suddenly to days of genial sunshine,
and groves and gardens burst into living greenery, and
rang with song, his heart was caught into the general joy.
Southey was not without a presentiment that his young
dodo would improve.   Soon her premature activity of eye
and spirits troubled him, and he tried, while cherishing
her, to put a guard upon his heart.   " I did not mean to
trust my affections again on so frail a foundation — and
yet the young one takes me from my desk and makes
me talk nonsense as fluently as you perhaps can imagine."
When Sara Coleridge—not yet five years old, but already,
as she half believed, promised in marriage to Mr. De Quincey—returned after a short absence to Greta Hall, she saw
her baby cousin, sixteen months younger, and therefore
not yet marriageable, grown into a little girl very fair,
with thick golden hair, and round, rosy cheeks.   Edith
Southey inherited something of her father's looks and of
his swift intelligence; with her growing beauty of face
and limbs a growing excellence of inward nature kept
pace.   At twenty she was the " elegant cygnet " of Amelia
Opie's album verses,

> " 'Twas pleasant to meet
> And see thee, famed Swan of the Derwent's fair tide,
> With that elegant cygnet that floats by thy side "—

a compliment her father mischievously would not let her
Elegancy forget.   Those who would know her in the loveliness of youthful womanhood may turn to Wordsworth's

poem, *The Triad*, where she appears first of the three " sister nymphs " of Keswick and Rydal ; or, Hartley Coleridge's exquisite sonnet, *To a lofty beauty, from her poor kinsman :*

> " Methinks thy scornful mood,
> And bearing high of stately womanhood—
> Thy brow where Beauty sits to tyrannize
> O'er humble love, had made me sadly fear thee :
> For never sure was seen a royal bride,
> Whose gentleness gave grace to so much pride—
> My very thoughts would tremble to be near thee,
> But when I see thee by thy father's side
> Old times unqueen thee, and old loves endear thee."

But it is best of all to remember Southey's daughter in connexion with one letter of her father's. In 1805 he visited Scotland alone ; he had looked forward to carrying on the most cherished purpose of his life—the *History of Portugal*—among the libraries of Lisbon. But it would be difficult to induce Mrs. Southey to travel with the Edithling. Could he go alone ? The short absence in Scotland served to test his heart, and so to make his future clear : —

" I need not tell you, my own dear Edith, not to read my letters aloud till you have first of all seen what is written only for yourself. What I have now to say to you is, that having been eight days from home, with as little discomfort, and as little reason for discomfort, as a man can reasonably expect, I have yet felt so little comfortable, so great sense of solitariness, and so many homeward yearnings, that certainly I will not go to Lisbon without you ; a resolution which, if your feelings be at all like mine, will not displease you. If, on mature consideration, you think the inconvenience of a voyage more than you ought to submit to, I must be content to stay in England, as on my part it certainly is not worth while to sacrifice a year's happiness; for though not unhappy (my mind is too active and too well disciplined to yield to any such criminal weakness), still, without you I am not happy. But for your sake as well as my own, and for little Edith's sake, I will not consent to any separation; the growth of a year's love between her and me, if it please God that she should live, is a thing too delightful in itself, and too valuable in its consequences, both to her and me, to be given up for any light inconvenience either on your part or mine. An absence of a year would make her effectually forget me. . . . But of these things we will talk at leisure; only, dear, dear Edith, we must not part."

Such wisdom of the heart was justified; the year of growing love bore precious fruit. When Edith May was ten years old her father dedicated to her, in verses laden with a father's tenderest thoughts and feelings, his *Tale of Paraguay*. He recalls the day of her birth, the preceding sorrow for his first child, whose infant features have faded from him like a passing cloud; the gladness of that singing month of May; the seasons that followed during which he observed the dawning of the divine light in her eyes; the playful guiles by which he won from her repeated kisses: to him these ten years seem like yesterday; but to her they have brought discourse of reason, with the sense of time and change:—

> "And I have seen thine eyes suffused in grief
>   When I have said that with autumnal grey
>   The touch of old hath mark'd thy father's head;
> That even the longest day of life is brief,
> And mine is falling fast into the yellow leaf."

Other children followed, until a happy stir of life filled the house. Emma, the quietest of infants, whose voice

was seldom heard, and whose dark-grey eyes too seldom
shone in her father's study, slipped quietly out of the
world after a hand's-breadth of existence; but to Southey
she was no more really lost than the buried brother and
sister were to the cottage girl of Wordsworth's *We are
seven.* "I have five children," he says in 1809; "three
of them at home, and two under my mother's care in
heaven." Of all, the most radiantly beautiful was Isabel;
the most passionately loved was Herbert. "My other
two are the most perfect contrast you ever saw. Bertha,
whom I call Queen Henry the Eighth, from her likeness
to King Bluebeard, grows like Jonah's gourd, and is the
very picture of robust health; and little Kate hardly seems
to grow at all, though perfectly well—she is round as a
mushroom-button. Bertha, the bluff queen, is just as
grave as Kate is garrulous; they are inseparable playfel-
lows, and go about the house hand in hand."

Among the inmates of Greta Hall, to overlook Lord
Nelson and Bona Marietta, with their numerous successors,
would be a grave delinquency. To be a cat, was to be a
privileged member of the little republic to which Southey
gave laws. Among the fragments at the end of *The Doctor* will be found a Chronicle History of the Cattery of
Cat's Eden; and some of Southey's frolic letters are written as if his whole business in life were that of secretary
for feline affairs in Greta Hall. A house, he declared, is
never perfectly furnished for enjoyment unless there is in
it a child rising three years old and a kitten rising six
weeks; "kitten is in the animal world what the rosebud
is in the garden." Lord Nelson, an ugly specimen of the
streaked-carroty or Judas-coloured kind, yet withal a good
cat, affectionate, vigilant, and brave, was succeeded by Ma-
dame Bianchi, a beautiful and singular creature, white, with

a fine tabby tail; "her wild eyes were bright, and green as the Duchess de Cadaval's emerald necklace." She fled away with her niece Pulcheria on the day when good old Mrs. Wilson died; nor could any allurements induce the pair to domesticate themselves again. For some time a cloud of doom seemed to hang over Cat's Eden. Ovid and Virgil, Othello the Moor, and Pope Joan perished miserably. At last Fortune, as if to make amends for her unkindness, sent to Greta Hall almost together the never-to-be-enough-praised Rumpelstilzchen (afterwards raised for services against rats to be His Serene Highness the Archduke Rumpelstilzchen), and the equally-to-be-praised Hurly-burlybuss. With whom too soon we must close the catalogue.

The revenue to maintain this household was in the main won by Southey's pen. "It is a difficult as well as a delicate task," he wrote in the *Quarterly Review*, " to advise a youth of ardent mind and aspiring thoughts in the choice of a profession; but a wise man will have no hesitation in exhorting him to choose anything rather than literature. Better that he should seek his fortune before the mast, or with a musket on his shoulder and a knapsack on his back; better that he should follow the plough, or work at the loom or the lathe, or sweat over the anvil, than trust to literature as the only means of his support." Southey's own bent towards literature was too strong to be altered. But, while he accepted loyally the burdens of his profession as a man of letters, he knew how stout a back is needed to bear them month after month and year after year. Absolutely dependent on his pen he was at no time. His generous friend Wynn, upon coming of age, allowed him annually 160*l.*, until, in 1807, he was able to procure for Southey a Government pension for literary services amount-

ing, clear of taxes, to nearly the same sum. Southey had
as truly as any man the pride of independence, but he had
none of its vanity; there was no humiliation in accepting
a service from one whom friendship had made as close as
a brother. Men, he says, are as much better for the good
offices which they receive as for those they bestow; and his
own was no niggard hand. Knowing both to give and
to take, with him the remembrance that he owed much to
others was among the precious possessions of life which
bind us to our kind with bonds of sonship, not of slavery.
Of the many kindnesses which he received he never forgot
one. "Had it not been for your aid," he writes to Wynn,
forty years after their first meeting in Dean's Yard, "I
should have been irretrievably wrecked when I ran upon
the shoals, with all sail set, in the very outset of my voyage." And to another good old friend, who from his own
modest station applauded while Southey ran forward in
the race:—"Do you suppose, Cottle, that I have forgotten
those true and most essential acts of friendship which you
showed me when I stood most in need of them? Your
house was my house when I had no other. The very
money with which I bought my wedding-ring and paid my
marriage-fees was supplied by you. It was with your sisters I left Edith during my six months' absence, and for
the six months after my return it was from you that I
received, week by week, the little on which we lived, till I
was enabled to live by other means. It is not the settling
of a cash account that can cancel obligations like these.
You are in the habit of preserving your letters, and if you
were not, I would entreat you to preserve *this*, that it might
be seen hereafter. . . . My head throbs and my eyes burn
with these recollections. Good-night! my dear old friend
and benefactor."

5*

Anxiety about his worldly fortunes never cost Southey
a sleepless night. His disposition was always hopeful;
relying on Providence, he says, I could rely upon myself.
When he had little, he lived upon little, never spending
when it was necessary to spare; and his means grew with
his expenses. Business habits he had none; never in his
life did he cast up an account; but in a general way he
knew that money comes by honest toil and grows by diligent husbandry. Upon Mrs. Southey, who had an eye to
all the household outgoings, the cares of this life fell more
heavily. Sara Coleridge calls to mind her aunt as she
moved about Greta Hall intent on house affairs, "with her
fine figure and quietly commanding air." Alas! under
this gracious dignity of manner the wear and tear of life
were doing their work surely. Still, it was honest wear
and tear. "I never knew her to do an unkind act," says
Southey, "nor say an unkind word;" but when stroke
followed upon stroke of sorrow, they found her without
that elastic temper which rises and recovers itself. Until
the saddest of afflictions made her helpless, everything was
left to her management, and was managed so quietly and
well, that, except in times of sickness and bereavement, "I
had," writes her husband, "literally no cares." Thus free
from harass, Southey toiled in his library; he toiled not
for bread alone. but also for freedom. There were great
designs before him which, he was well aware, if ever realized, would make but a poor return to the household cof-
fer. To gain time and a vantage-ground for these, he was
content to yield much of his strength to work of tempo-
rary value, always contriving, however, to strike a mean in
this journeyman service between what was most and least
akin to his proper pursuits. When a parcel of books arrived from the *Annual Review*, he groaned in spirit over

the sacrifice of time; but patience! it is, after all, better, he would reflect, than pleading in a court of law; better than being called up at midnight to a patient; better than calculating profit and loss at a counter; better, in short, than anything but independence. "I am a quiet, patient, easy-going hack of the mule breed"—he writes to Grosvenor Bedford—"regular as clock-work in my pace, sure-footed, bearing the burden which is laid on me, and only obstinate in choosing my own path. If Gifford could see me by this fireside, where, like Nicodemus, one candle suffices me in a large room, he would see a man in a coat 'still more threadbare than his own,' when he wrote his 'Imitation,' working hard and getting little—a bare maintenance, and hardly that; writing poems and history for posterity with his whole heart and soul; one daily progressive in learning, not so learned as he is poor, not so poor as proud, not so proud as happy. Grosvenor, there is not a lighter-hearted nor a happier man upon the face of this wide world." When these words were written, Herbert stood by his father's side; it was sweet to work that his boy might have his play-time glad and free.

The public estimate of Southey's works as expressed in pounds, shillings, and pence, was lowest where he held that it ought to have been highest. For the *History of Brazil*, a work of stupendous toil, which no one in England could have produced save Southey himself, he had not received, after eight years, as much as for a single article in the *Quarterly Review*. *Madoc*, the pillar, as he supposed, on which his poetical fame was to rest; *Madoc*, which he dismissed with an awed feeling, as if in it he were parting with a great fragment of his life, brought its author, after twelve months' sales, the sum of 3*l*. 17*s*. 1*d*. On the other hand, for his *Naval Biography*, which interested him

less than most of his works, and which was undertaken
after hesitation, he was promised five hundred guineas a
volume.   Notwithstanding his unwearied exertions, his
modest scale of expenditure, and his profitable connexion
with the *Quarterly Review*—for an important article he
would receive 100*l*.—he never had a year's income in advance until that year, late in his life, in which Sir Robert
Peel offered him a baronetcy.   In 1818, the lucky pay-
ment of a bad debt enabled him to buy 300*l*. in the
Three-per-cents.   " I have 100*l*. already there," he writes,
" and shall then be worth 12*l*. per annum."   By 1821
this sum had grown to 625*l*., the gatherings of half a
life-time.   In that year his friend John May, whose acquaintance he had made in Portugal, and to whose kindness he was a debtor, suffered the loss of his fortune.   As
soon as Southey had heard the state of affairs, his decision
was formed.   " By this post," he tells his friend, " I write
to Bedford, desiring that he will transfer to you 625*l*. in
the Three-per-cents.   I wish it was more, and that I had
more at my command in any way.   I shall in the spring,
if I am paid for the first volume of my History as soon as
it is finished.   One hundred I should, at all events, have
sent you then.   It shall be as much more as I receive."
And he goes on in cheery words to invite John May to
break away from business and come to Keswick, there to
lay in " a pleasant store of recollections which in all moods
of mind are wholesome."   One rejoices that Southey,
poor of worldly goods, knew the happiness of being so
simply and nobly generous.

Blue and white china, mediæval ivories, engravings by
the Little Masters, Chippendale cabinets, did not excite
pining desire in Southey's breast; yet in one direction
he indulged the passion of a collector.   If, with respect to

any of " the things independent of the will," he showed a
want of moderation unworthy of his discipleship to Epictetus, it was assuredly with respect to books.   Before he
possessed a fixed home, he was already moored to his folios; and when once he was fairly settled at Keswick,
many a time the carriers on the London road found their
lading the larger by a weighty packet on its way to Greta
Hall.   Never did he run north or south for a holiday,
but the inevitable parcel preceded or followed his return.
Never did he cross to the Continent but a bulkier bale arrived in its own good time, enclosing precious things.   His
morality, in all else void of offence, here yielded to the
seducer.   It is thought that Southey was in the main honest; but if Dirk Hatteraick had run ashore a hundred-
weight of the Acta Sanctorum duty-free, the king's laureate was not the man to set the sharks upon him; and it
is to be feared that the pattern of probity, the virtuous
Southey himself, might in such circumstances be found,
under cover of night, lugging his prize landwards from its
retreat beneath the rocks.   Unquestionably, at one time
certain parcels from Portugal — only of such a size as
could be carried under the arm — were silently brought
ashore to the defrauding of the revenue, and somehow
found their way, by-and-by, to Greta Hall.   "We maintain a trade," says the Governor of the Strangers' House
in Bacon's philosophical romance, " not for gold, silver, or
jewels, nor for silks, nor for spices, nor any other com-
modity of matter, but only for God's first creature, which
was *light*."   Such, too, was Southey's trade, and he held
that God's first creature is free to travel unchallenged by
revenue-cutter.

" Why, Montesinos," asks the ghostly Sir Thomas More
in one of Southey's *Colloquies*, " with these books and the

delight you take in their constant society, what have you
to covet or desire?" "Nothing," is the answer, ". . . except more books."   When Southey, in 1805, went to see
Walter Scott, it occurred to him in Edinburgh that, having
had neither new coat nor hat since little Edith was born,
he must surely be in want of both; and here, in the metropolis of the North, was an opportunity of arraying himself to his desire.   "Howbeit," he says, "on considering
the really respectable appearance which my old ones made
for a traveller — and considering, moreover, that as learning was better than house or land, it certainly must be
much better than fine clothes — I laid out all my money
in books, and came home to wear out my old wardrobe
in the winter."   De Quincey called Southey's library his
wife, and in a certain sense it was wife and mistress and
mother to him.   The presence and enjoying of his books
was not the sole delight they afforded; there was also the
pursuit, the surprisal, the love-making or wooing.   And at
last, in his hours of weakness, once more a little child, he
would walk slowly round his library, looking at his cherished volumes, taking them down mechanically, and when
he could no longer read, pressing them to his lips.   In
happier days the book-stalls of London knew the tall figure, the rapid stride, the quick-seeing eye, the eager fingers.   Lisbon, Paris, Milan, Amsterdam, contributed to
the rich confusion that, from time to time, burdened the
floors of library and bedrooms and passages in Greta Hall.
Above all, he was remembered at Brussels by that best
of bookmen, Verbeyst.   What mattered it that Verbeyst
was a sloven, now receiving his clients with gaping shirt,
and now with stockingless feet?   Did he not duly honour letters, and had he not 300,000 volumes from which
to choose?   If in a moment of prudential weakness one

failed to carry off such a treasure as the *Monumenta Boi-
ca* or Colgar's *Irish Saints*, there was a chance that in
Verbeyst's vast store-house the volume might lurk for a
year or two.   And Verbeyst loved his books, only less
than he loved his handsome, good-natured wife, who for
a liberal customer would fetch the bread and burgundy.
Henry Taylor dwelt in Robert Southey's heart of hearts;
but let not Henry Taylor treasonably hint that Verbeyst,
the prince of booksellers, had not a prince's politeness of
punctuality.   If sundry books promised had not arrived,
it was because they were not easily procured; moreover,
the good-natured wife had died — *bien des malheurs*, and
Verbeyst's heart was fallen into a lethargy.   " Think ill of
our fathers which are in the Row, think ill of John Murray, think ill of Colburn, think ill of the whole race of
bibliopoles, except Verbeyst, who is always to be thought
of with liking and respect."   And when the bill of lading,
coming slow but sure, announced that saints and chron-
iclers and poets were on their way, " by this day month,"
wrote Southey, " they will probably be here ; then shall I
be happier than if his Majesty King George the Fourth
were to give orders that I should be clothed in purple, and
sleep upon gold, and have a chain upon my neck, and sit
next him because of my wisdom, and be called his cousin."

Thus the four thousand volumes, which lay piled about
the library when Southey first gathered his possessions
together, grew and grew, year after year, until the grand
total mounted up to eight, to ten, to fourteen thousand.
Now Kirke White's brother Neville sends him a gift of
Sir William Jones's works, thirteen volumes, in binding
of bewildering loveliness.   Now Landor ships from some
Italian port a chest containing treasures of less dubious
value than the Raffaelles and Leonardos, with which he lib-

erally supplied his art-loving friends. Oh, the joy of
opening such a chest; of discovering the glorious folios;
of glancing with the shy amorousness of first desire at
title-page and colophon; of growing familiarity; of tracing out the history suggested by book-plate or autograph;
of finding a lover's excuses for cropped margin, or water-
stain, or worm-hole! Then the calmer happiness of arranging his favourites on new shelves; of taking them
down again, after supper, in the season of meditation and
currant-rum; and of wondering for which among his father's books Herbert will care most when all of them shall
be his own. "It would please you," Southey writes to his
old comrade, Bedford, "to see such a display of literary
wealth, which is at once the pride of my eye, and the joy
of my heart, and the food of my mind; indeed, more than
metaphorically, meat, drink, and clothes for me and mine.
I verily believe that no one in my station was ever so rich
before, and I am very sure that no one in any station had
ever a more thorough enjoyment of riches of any kind or
in any way."

Southey's Spanish and Portuguese collection—if Heber's
great library be set aside—was probably the most remarkable gathering of such books in the possession of any
private person in this country. It included several manuscripts, some of which were displayed with due distinction upon brackets. Books in white and gold—vellum or
parchment bound, with gilt lettering in the old English
type which Southey loved—were arranged in effective positions pyramid-wise. Southey himself had learned the
mystery of book-binding, and from him his daughters acquired that art; the ragged volumes were decently clothed
in coloured cotton prints; these, presenting a strange
patch-work of colours, quite filled one room, which was

known as the Cottonian Library. "Paul," a book-room on
the ground-floor, had been so called because "Peter," the
organ-room, was robbed to fit it with books. "Paul is
a great comfort to us, and being dressed up with Peter's
property, makes a most respectable appearance, and receives
that attention which is generally shown to the youngest
child. The study has not actually been Petered on Paul's
account, but there has been an exchange negotiated which
we think is for their mutual advantage. Twenty gilt volumes, from under the 'Beauties of England and Wales,'
have been marched down-stairs rank and file, and their
place supplied by the long set of Lope de Vega with green
backs."

Southey's books, as he assures his ghostly monitor in
the *Colloquies*, were not drawn up on his shelves for display, however much the pride of the eye might be gratified
in beholding them; they were on actual service. Generations might pass away before some of them would again
find a reader; in their mountain home they were prized
and known as perhaps they never had been known before.
Not a few of the volumes had been cast up from the wreck
of family or convent libraries during the Revolution.
"Yonder Acta Sanctorum belonged to the Capuchines at
Ghent. This book of St. Bridget's Revelations, in which
not only all the initial letters are illuminated, but every
capital throughout the volume was coloured, came from
the Carmelite Nunnery at Bruges. . . . Here are books
from Colbert's library; here others from the Lamoignon
one. . . . Yonder Chronicle History of King D. Manoel, by
Damiam de Goes; and yonder General History of Spain,
by Esteban de Garibay, are signed by their respective authors. . . . This Copy of Casaubon's Epistles was sent to
me from Florence by Walter Landor. He had perused it

H   8

carefully, and to that perusal we are indebted for one of
the most pleasing of his Conversations. . . . Here is a book
with which Lauderdale amused himself, when Cromwell
kept him in prison in Windsor Castle. . . . Here I possess
these gathered treasures of time, the harvest of many generations, laid up in my garners: and when I go to the
window, there is the lake, and the circle of the mountains,
and the illimitable sky."

Not a few of his books were dead, and to live among
these was like living among the tombs; "Behold, this also
is vanity," Southey makes confession. But when Sir Thomas questions, "Has it proved to you 'vexation of spirit'
also?" the Cumberland mountain-dweller breaks forth:
"Oh no! for never can any man's life have been passed
more in accord with his own inclinations, nor more an-
swerably to his desires. Excepting that peace which,
through God's infinite mercy, is derived from a higher
source, it is to literature, humanly speaking, that I am be-
holden, not only for the means of subsistence, but for
every blessing which I enjoy; health of mind and activity
of mind, contentment, cheerfulness, continual employment,
and therefore continual pleasure. *Suavissima vita indies
sentire se fieri meliorem;* and this, as Bacon has said and
Clarendon repeated, is the benefit that a studious man en-
joys in retirement." Such a grave gladness underlay all
Southey's frolic moods, and in union with a clear-sighted
acceptance of the conditions of human happiness—its inevitable shocks, its transitory nature as far as it belongs to
man's life on earth—made up part of his habitual temper.

Southey coursed from page to page with a greyhound's
speed; a tiny *s* pencilled in the margin served to indicate
what might be required for future use. Neatness he had
learnt from Miss Tyler long ago; and by experience he ac-

quired his method. On a slip of paper which served as
marker he would note the pages to which he needed to return. In the course of a few hours he had classified and
arranged everything in a book which it was likely he
would ever want. A reference to the less important passages sufficed; those of special interest were transcribed
by his wife, or one of his daughters, or more frequently
by Southey himself; finally, these transcripts were brought
together in packets under such headings as would make it
easy to discover any portion of their contents.

Such was his ordinary manner of eviscerating an author,
but it was otherwise with the writers of his affection. On
some—such as Jackson and Jeremy Taylor—" he *fed*," as
he expressed it, " slowly and carefully, dwelling on the
page, and taking in its contents, deeply and deliberately,
like an epicure with his wine ' searching the subtle fla-
vour.'" Such chosen writers remained for all times and
seasons faithful and cherished friends :—

> " With them I take delight in weal,
>   And seek relief in woe;
> And while I understand and feel
>   How much to them I owe,
> My cheeks have often been bedewed
>   With tears of thankful gratitude."

" If I were confined to a score of English books," says
Southey, " Sir Thomas Browne would, I think, be one of
them ; nay, probably it would be one if the selection were
cut down to twelve. My library, if reduced to those
bounds, would consist of Shakspeare, Chaucer, Spenser,
and Milton ; Jackson, Jeremy Taylor, and South ; Isaac
Walton, Sidney's Arcadia, Fuller's Church History, and
Sir Thomas Browne ; and what a wealthy and well-stored

mind would that man have, what an inexhaustible reser-
voir, what a Bank of England to draw upon for profitable
thoughts and delightful associations, who should have fed
upon them!" It must have gone hard with Southey, in
making out this list, to exclude Clarendon, and doubtless
if the choice were not limited to books written in English,
the Utopia would have urged its claim to admission. With
less difficulty he could skip the whole of the eighteenth
century. From *Samson Agonistes* to *The Task*, there was
no English poem which held a foremost place in his es-
teem. Berkeley and Butler he valued highly; but Robert
South seemed to him the last of the race of the giants.
An ancestral connection with Locke was not a source of
pride to Southey; he respected neither the philosopher's
politics nor his metaphysics; still, it is pleasant, he says, to
hear of somebody between one's self and Adam who has
left a name.

Four volumes of what are called Southey's *Commonplace Books* have been published, containing some three
thousand double-column pages; and these are but a selection from the total mass of his transcripts. It is impossible to give a notion of a miscellany drawn from so wide-
ranging a survey of poetry, biography, history, travels, to-
pography, divinity, not in English alone, but also in Latin,
French, Italian, Spanish, Portuguese. Yet certain main
lines can be traced which give some meaning to this huge
accumulation. It is easy to perceive that the collector
wrought under an historical bias, and that social, literary,
and ecclesiastical history were the directions in which the
historical tendency found its play. Such work of transcribing, though it did not rest Southey's hand, was a relief to his mind after the excitement of composition, and
some of it may pass for a kind of busy idleness; but most

of his transcripts were made with a definite purpose—that of furnishing materials for work either actually accomplished or still in prospect, when at last the brain grew dull and the fingers slack. "I am for ever making collections," he writes, "and storing up materials which may not come into use till the Greek Calends. And this I have been doing for five-and-twenty years! It is true that I draw daily upon my hoards, and should be poor without them; but in prudence I ought now to be working up those materials rather than adding to so much dead stock." When Ticknor visited him in 1819, Southey opened for the young American his great bundles of manuscript materials for the *History of Portugal*, and the *History of the Portuguese East Indies*. Southey had charmed him by the kindness of his reception; by the air of culture and of goodness in his home; by his talk, bright and eager, "for the quickness of his mind expresses itself in the fluency of his utterance; and yet he is ready upon almost any subject that can be proposed to him, from the extent of his knowledge." And now, when Ticknor saw spread before him the evidence of such unexampled industry, a kind of bewilderment took possession of him. "Southey," he writes in his diary, "is certainly an extraordinary man, one of those whose characters I find it difficult to comprehend, because I hardly know how such elements can be brought together, such rapidity of mind with such patient labour and wearisome exactness, so mild a disposition with so much nervous excitability, and a poetical talent so elevated with such an immense mass of minute, dull learning."

If Ticknor had been told that this was due to Epictetus, it might have puzzled him still more; but it is certain that only through the strenuous appliance of will to the formation of character could Southey have grown to be what he

was. He had early been possessed by the belief that he
must not permit himself to become the slave or the victim
of sensibility, but that in the little world of man there are
two powers ruling by a Divine right — reason and conscience, in loyal obedience to which lies our highest freedom. Then, too, the circumstances of his life prompted
him to self-mastery and self-management. That he should
every day overtake a vast amount of work, was not left to
his choosing or declining—it was a matter of necessity ; to
accomplish this, he must get all possible advantage out of
his rapidity of intellect and his energy of feeling, and at
the same time he must never put an injurious strain on
these. It would not do for Southey to burn away to-day
in some white flame of excitement the nerve which he
needed for use to-morrow. He could not afford to pass
a sleepless night. If his face glowed or his brain throb-
bed, it was a warning that he had gone far enough. His
very susceptibility to nervous excitement rendered caution
the more requisite. William Taylor had compared him
to the mimosa. Hazlitt remembered him with a quivering lip, a hectic flush upon his cheek, a roving fire in his
eye, a falcon glance, a look at once aspiring and dejected.
Crabb Robinson found in him a likeness to Shelley.
Humphry Davy had proved the fineness of his sensibility
by that odd neurometer, the nitrous oxide. " The truth
is," writes Southey, " that though some persons, whose
knowledge of me is scarcely skin-deep, suppose I have no
nerves, because I have great self-control as far as regards
the surface, if it were not for great self-management, and
what may be called a strict intellectual regimen, I should
very soon be in a deplorable state of what is called nervous
disease, and this would have been the case any time during
the last twenty years." And again : " A man had better

break a bone, or even lose a limb, than shake his nervous system. I, who never talk about my nerves (and am supposed to have none by persons who see as far into me as they do into a stone wall), know this." Southey could not afford to play away his health at hazard, and then win it back in the lounge of some foreign watering-place. His plan, on the contrary, was to keep it, and to think about it as little as possible. A single prescription sufficed for a life-time —*In labore quies.* "I think I may lay claim," he says, "to the praise of self-management both in body and mind without paying too much attention to either—exercising a diseased watchfulness, or playing any tricks with either." It would not have been difficult for Southey, with such a temperament as his, to have wrecked himself at the outset of his career. With beautiful foiled lives of young men Southey had a peculiar sympathy. But the gods sometimes give white hairs as an aureole to their favoured ones. Perhaps, on the whole, for him it was not only more prudent but also more chivalrous to study to be quiet; to create a home for those who looked to him for security; to guard the happiness of tender women; to make smooth ways for the feet of little children; to hold hands in old age with the friends of his youth; to store his mind with treasures of knowledge; to strengthen and chasten his own heart; to grow yearly in love for his country and her venerable heritage of manners, virtue, laws; to add to her literature the outcome of an adult intellect and character; and having fought a strenuous and skilful fight, to fall as one whose sword an untimely stroke has shattered in his hand.

CHAPTER V.

THE texture of Southey's life was so uniform, the round from morning till night repeated itself with so much regularity, that one day may stand as representative of a thousand. We possess his record of how the waking hours went by when he was about thirty years old, and a similar record written when he was twice that age. His surroundings had changed in the mean time, and he himself had changed; the great bare room which he used from the first as a study, fresh plastered in 1804, with the trowel-lines on the ceiling pierced by the flaws of winter, containing two chairs and a little table—" God help me !" he exclaims, "I look in it like a cock-robin in a church " —this room had received, long before 1834, its lining of comely books, its white and gold pyramids, its brackets, its cherished portraits. The occupant of the study had the same spare frame, the same aspect of lightness and of strength, the same full eyebrows shadowing the dark-brown eyes, the same variously expressive muscular mouth; the youthful wildness in his countenance had given place to a thoughtful expression, and the abundant hair still clustering over his great brow was snowy white. Whatever had changed, his habits—though never his tyrants— remained, with some variations in detail, the same. " My actions," he writes to a friend not very long after his arrival in Keswick, " are as regular as those of St. Dunstan's quarter - boys. Three pages of history after breakfast (equivalent to five in small quarto printing); then to transcribe and copy for the press, or to make my selections and biographies, or what else suits my humour till dinner-time; from dinner to tea I read, write letters, see the newspaper, and very often indulge in a siesta — for sleep agrees with me. . . . After tea I go to poetry, and correct, and rewrite, and copy till I am tired, and then turn to anything else till supper; and this is my life— which, if it be not a very merry one, is yet as happy as heart could wish." " See how the day is disposed of!" begins the later record; " I get out of bed as the clock strikes six, and shut the house-door after me as it strikes seven.[1] After two hours with Davies, home to breakfast, after which Cuthbert engages me till about half-past ten, and when the post brings no letters that either interest or trouble me (for of the latter I have many), by eleven I have done with the newspaper, and can then set about what is properly the business of the day. But letters are often to be written, and I am liable to frequent interruptions; so that there are not many mornings in which I can command from two to three unbroken hours at the desk. At two I take my daily walk, be the weather what it may, and when the weather permits, with a book in my hand; dinner at four, read about half an hour; then take to the sofa with a different book, and after a few pages get my soundest sleep, till summoned to tea at six. My best time during the winter is by candle-light; twilight

---

[1] *I. e.*, to go to Davies' lodgings; Davies, Dr. Bell's Secretary, was engaged in arranging a vast accumulation of papers with a view to forwarding Southey in his *Life of Bell*.

interferes with it a little; and in the season of company
I can never count upon an evening's work. Supper at
half-past nine, after which I read an hour, and then to
bed. The greatest part of my miscellaneous work is done
in the odds and ends of time."

It was part of Southey's regimen to carry on several
works at once; this he found to be economy of time, and
he believed it necessary for the preservation of his health.
Whenever one object entirely occupied his attention, it
haunted him, oppressed him, troubled his dreams. The
remedy was simple—to do one thing in the morning, another in the evening. To lay down poetry and presently
to attack history seems feasible, and no ill policy for one
who is forced to take all he can out of himself; but
Southey would turn from one poetical theme to another,
and could day by day advance with a pair of epics. This
was a source of unfailing wonder to Landor. " When I
write a poem," he says, "my heart and all my feelings are
upon it. . . . High poems will not admit flirtation." Little by little was Southey's way, and so he got on with
many things. " Last night," he writes to Bedford, "I began the Preface [to *Specimens of English Poets*]—huz-
za! And now, Grosvenor, let me tell you what I have to
do. I am writing—1. *The History of Portugal;* 2. *The
Chronicle of the Cid;* 3. *The Curse of Kehama;* 4. *Espriella's Letters.* Look you, all these *I am* writing. . . .
By way of interlude comes in this preface. Don't swear,
and bid me do one thing at a time. I tell you I can't
afford to do one thing at a time—no, nor two neither;
and it is only by doing many things that I contrive to do
so much: for I cannot work long together at anything
without hurting myself, and so I do everything by heats;
then, by the time I am tired of one, my inclination for

another is come round." A strong, deliberate energy, accordingly, is at the back of all Southey's work; but not that blind creative rapture which will have its own way, and leaves its subject weak but appeased. "In the daytime I laboured," says Landor, "and at night unburdened my soul, shedding many tears. My *Tiberius* has so shaken me at last that the least thing affects me violently." Southey shrank back from such agitations. A great Elizabethan poet is described by one of his contemporaries as one standing

> "Up to the chin in the Pierian flood."

Southey did not wade so far; he stepped down calmly until the smooth waters touched his waist; dipped seven times, and returned to the bank. It was a beautiful and an elevating rite; but the waves sing with lyric lips only in the midmost stream; and he who sings with them, and as swift as they, need not wonder if he sink after a time, faint, breathless, delighted.

Authorship, it must be remembered, was Southey's trade, the business of his life, and this, at least, he knew how to conduct well. To be a prophet and call down flame from heaven, and disappear in a whirlwind and a chariot of fire, is sublime; but prophets can go in the strength of a single meal for more days and nights than one would choose to name in this incredulous age, and, if they eat, there are ravens to bring them food. No ravens brought loaves to Greta Hall; and Southey had an unprophet-like craving for the creature comforts of beef and bread, for wine if it might be had, and at supper for one meditative tumbler of punch or black-currant rum. Besides, what ravens were ever pledged to feed a prophet's sisters-in-law, or his nephews and nieces? Let it be praise enough for much

of Southey's performance that he did good work in work-
manlike fashion. To shift knowledge into more conven-
ient positions is to render no unimportant service to mankind. In the gathering of facts, Southey was both swift
and patient in an extraordinary degree ; he went often
alone, and he went far; in the art of exposition he was
unsurpassed ; and his fine moral feeling and profound
sympathy with elementary justice created, as De Quincey
has observed, a soul under what else might well be denom-
inated, Miltonically, " the ribs of death." From the mending of his pens to the second reading aloud of his proof-
sheets, attending as he read to the fall of each word upon
the ear, Southey had a diligent care for everything that
served to make his work right. He wrote at a moderate
pace ; re-wrote ; wrote a third time if it seemed desirable ;
corrected with minute supervision. He accomplished so
much, not because he produced with unexampled rapidity,
but because he worked regularly, and never fell into a
mood of apathy or ennui. No periods of tempestuous
vacancy lay between his periods of patient labour. One
work always overlapped another—thus, that first idle day,
the begetter of so many idle descendants, never came.
But let us hear the craftsman giving a lesson in the knack
of authorship to his brother, Dr. Henry Southey, who has
a notion of writing something on the Crusades :

" Now then, supposing that you will seriously set about
the *Crusades*, I will give you such directions in the art of historical book-keeping as may save time and facilitate labour.

" Make your writing-books in foolscap quarto, and write
on only one side of a leaf; draw a line down the margin,
marking off space enough for your references, which should
be given at the end of every paragraph ; noting page, book,
or chapter of the author referred to. This minuteness is now

demanded, and you will yourself find it useful; for, in transcribing or in correcting proofs, it is often requisite to turn to
the original authorities.   Take the best author; that is to
say, the one that has written most at length of all the *original*
authors, upon the particular point of time on which you are
employed, and draw up your account from him; then, on the
opposite page, correct and amplify this from every other who
has written on the same subject.   This page should be divided into two columns, one of about two-thirds of its breadth,
the other the remaining one.   You are thus enabled to *add*
to your *additions.*

"One of these books you should have for your geography;
that is to say, for collecting descriptions of all the principal
scenes of action (which must be done from books of travels),
their situation, their strength, their previous history, and in
the notes, their present state.   [Another book—he adds in a
subsequent letter — you must keep for the bibliography of
your subject.]

"These descriptions you can insert in their proper places
when you transcribe.   Thus, also, you should collect accounts
of the different tribes and dynasties which you have occasion
to mention.   In this manner the information which is only
to be got at piecemeal, and oftentimes incidentally, when you
are looking for something else, is brought together with least
trouble, and almost imperceptibly.

"All relative matter not absolutely essential to the subject
should go in the form of supplementary notes, and these you
may make as amusing as you please, the more so, and the
more curious, the better.   Much trouble is saved by writing
them on separate bits of paper, each the half of a quarter of
a foolscap sheet—numbering them, and making an index of
them; in this manner they are ready for use when they are
wanted.

"It was some time before I fell unto this system of book-
keeping, and I believe no better can be desired.   A Welsh
triad might comprehend all the rules of style.   Say what you

have to say as *perspicuously* as possible, as *briefly* as possible,
and as *rememberably* as possible, and take no other thought
about it.   Omit none of those little circumstances which
give life to narration, and bring old manners, old feelings,
and old times before your eyes."

Winter was Southey's harvest season.   Then for weeks
no visitor knocked at Greta Hall, except perhaps Mr.
Wordsworth, who had plodded all the way from Rydal on
his indefatigable legs.   But in summer interruptions were
frequent, and Southey, who had time for everything, had
time to spare not only for friends but for strangers.   The
swarm of lakers was, indeed, not what it is now-a-days, but
to a studious man it was, perhaps, not less formidable.   By
Gray's time the secret of the lakes had been found out;
and if the visitors were fewer, they were less swift upon
the wing, and their rank or fame often entitled them to
particular attention.   Coroneted coaches rolled into Keswick, luggage-laden; the American arrived sometimes to
make sure that Derwentwater would not be missed out of
Lake Michigan, sometimes to see King George's laureate;
and cultured Americans were particularly welcome to
Southey.   Long-vacation reading-parties from Oxford and
Cambridge—known among the good Cumberland folk as
the "cathedrals"—made Keswick a resort.   Well for
them if, provided with an introduction, they were invited
to dine at Greta Hall, were permitted to gaze on the
choice old Spaniards, and to converse with the laureate's
stately Edith and her learned cousin.   Woe to them if,
after the entanglements of a Greek chorus or descriptions
of the temperate man and the magnanimous man, they
sought to restore their tone by a cat-worrying expedition
among the cottages of Keswick.   Southey's cheek glowed,
his eye darkened and flashed, if he chanced to witness cru-

elty; some of the Cambridge "cathedrals" who received
a letter concerning cats in July, 1834, may still bear the
mark of its leaded thong in their moral fibre, and be the
better for possessing Southey's sign-manual.

A young step-child of Oxford visited Keswick in the
winter of 1811–12, and sought the acquaintance of the
author of *Thalaba*. Had Southey been as intolerant or
as unsympathetic as some have represented him, he could
not have endured the society of one so alien in opinion
and so outspoken as Shelley. But courtesy, if it were
nothing more, was at least part of Southey's self-respect;
his intolerance towards persons was, in truth, towards a
certain ideal, a certain group of opinions; when hand
touched hand and eye met eye, all intolerance vanished,
and he was open to every gracious attraction of character
and manner. There was much in Shelley that could not
fail to interest Southey; both loved poetry, and both felt
the proud, secluded grandeur of Landor's verse; both loved
men, and thought the world wants mending, though their
plans of reform might differ. That Shelley was a rebel
expelled from Oxford did not shock Southey, who himself had been expelled from Westminster and rejected at
Christ Church. Shelley's opinions were crude and violent,
but their spirit was generous, and such opinions held by
a youth in his teens generally mean no more than that
his brain is working and his heart ardent. Shelley's rash
marriage reminded Southey of another marriage, celebrated
at Bristol some fifteen years ago, which proved that rash-
ness is not always folly. The young man's admiration of
Thalaba spoke well for him; and certainly during the
earlier weeks of their intercourse there was on Shelley's
part a becoming deference to one so much his superior in
years and in learning, deference to one who had achieved

much while Shelley still only dreamed of achievement.
Southey thought he saw in the revolutionary enthusiast
an image of his former self. " Here," he says, " is a man
at Keswick who acts upon me as my own ghost would do.
He is just what I was in 1794. His name is Shelley, son
to the member for Shoreham. . . . At present he has got
to the Pantheistic stage of philosophy, and in the course
of a week I expect he will be a Berkeleyan, for I have put
him upon a course of Berkeley. It has surprised him a
good deal to meet, for the first time in his life, with a man
who perfectly understands him and does him full justice.
I tell him that all the difference between us is that he is
nineteen and I am thirty-seven; and I daresay it will not
be very long before I shall succeed in convincing him that
he may be a true philosopher and do a great deal of good
with 6000l. a year; the thought of which troubles him a
great deal more at present than ever the want of sixpence
(for I have known such a want) did me." There were
other differences between Robert Southey and the incon-
stant star that passed by Greta Hall than that of years.
Southey had quickly learned to put a bound to his desires,
and within that bound to work out for himself a possession of measureless worth. It seemed to him part of a
man's virtue to adhere loyally to the bond signed for each
of us when we enter life. Is our knowledge limited—
then let us strive within those limits. Can we never lay
hands on the absolute good—then let us cherish the good
things that are ours. Do we hold our dearest possessions
on a limited tenure—that is hard, but is it not in the
bond? How faint a loyalty is his who merely yields obedience perforce! let us rather cast in our will, unadulterate
and whole, with that of our divine Leader; *sursum corda*
—there is a heaven above. But Shelley—the nympholept

of some radiant ante-natal sphere—fled through his brief
years ever in pursuit of his lost lady of light; and for him
loyalty to the bond of life seemed to mean a readiness to
forget all things, however cherished, so soon as they had
fulfilled their service of speeding him on towards the un-
attainable. It could not but be that men living under
rules so diverse should before long find themselves far
asunder. But they parted in 1812 in no spirit of ill-will.
Southey was already a state-pensioner and a champion of
the party of order in the *Quarterly Review;* this did not
prevent the young apostle of liberty and fraternity from
entering his doors, and enjoying Mrs. Southey's tea-cakes.
Irish affairs were earnestly discussed; but Southey, who
had written generously of Emmett both in his verse and
in the *Quarterly*, could not be hostile to one whose illu-
sions were only over-sanguine; and while the veritable
Southey was before Shelley's eyes, he could not discern
the dull hireling, the venomous apostate, the cold-blooded
assassin, of freedom conjured up by Byron and others to
bear Southey's name.

Three years later Shelley presented his *Alastor* to the
laureate, and Southey duly acknowledged the gift. The
elder poet was never slow to recognize genius in young
men, but conduct was to him of higher importance than
genius; he deplored some acts in Shelley's life which
seemed to result directly from opinions professed at Keswick in 1811—opinions then interpreted as no more than
the disdain of checks felt by every spirited boy. Southey
heard no more from him until a letter came from Pisa in-
quiring whether Shelley's former entertainer at Keswick
were his recent critic of the *Quarterly Review*, with added
comments, courteous but severe, on Southey's opinions.
The reply was that Southey had not written the paper, and

had never in any of his writings alluded to Shelley in any
way. A second letter followed on each side, the elder
man pleading, exhorting, warning; the younger justifying
himself, and returning to the attack. "There the correspondence ended. On Shelley's part it was conducted with
the courtesy which was natural to him; on mine, in the
spirit of one who was earnestly admonishing a fellow-
creature."

Much of Southey's time—his most valued possession—
was given to his correspondents. Napoleon's plan of an-
swering letters, according to Bourrienne, was to let them
lie unopened for six weeks, by which time nine out of ten
had answered themselves, or had been answered by history. Coleridge's plan—says De Quincey—was shorter;
he opened none, and answered none. To answer all forthwith was the habit of Southey. Thinking doubtless of
their differences in such minor moralities of life, Coleridge
writes of his brother-in-law:—"Always employed, his
friends find him always at leisure. No less punctual in
trifles than steadfast in the performance of highest duties,
he inflicts none of those small pains which irregular men
scatter about them, and which in the aggregate so often
become formidable obstacles both to happiness and utility;
while, on the contrary, he bestows all the pleasures and in-
spires all that ease of mind on those around or connected
with him, which perfect consistency and (if such a word
might be framed) absolute *reliability*, equally in small as
in great concerns, cannot but inspire and bestow; when
this, too, is softened without being weakened by kindness
and gentleness." Odd indeed were some of the communi-
cations for which the poet-laureate, the Tory reformer, and
the loyal son of the Church was the mark. Now a clergyman writes to furnish him with Scriptural illustrations of

Thalaba; now another clergyman favours him with an
ingenious parallel between Kehama and Nebuchadnezzar;
now some anonymous person seriously urges on Southey
his duty of making a new version of the Psalms, and laying it before the King to be approved and appointed to
be sung in churches; now a lunatic poet desires his brother to procure for his title-page the names of Messrs. Longman and Rees; now a poor woman, wife to a blind Homer,
would have him led carefully to the summit of Parnassus;
now a poor French devil volunteers to translate *Roderick*
if the author will have the goodness to send him a copy
—even a defective copy — which he pledges himself re-
ligiously to return; now a Yankee, who keeps an exhibition
at Philadelphia, modestly asks for Southey's painted portrait, "which is very worthy a place in my collection;"
now a herdsman in the vale of Clwyd requests permission
to send specimens of prose and verse—his highest ambition is the acquaintance of learned men; now the Rev.
Peter Hall begs to inform Southey that he has done more
harm to the cause of religion than any writer of the age;
now a lover requests him to make an acrostic on the name
of a young lady—the lover's rival has beaten him in writing verses; enclosed is the honorarium. Southey's ami-
ability at this point gave way; he did not write the acrostic, and the money he spent on blankets for poor women
in Keswick. A society for the suppression of albums was
proposed by Southey; yet sometimes he was captured in
the gracious mood. Samuel Simpson, of Liverpool, begs
for a few lines in his handwriting "to fill a vacancy in his
collection of autographs, without which his series must remain for ever most incomplete." The laureate replies:

"Inasmuch as you Sam, a descendant of Sim,
   For collecting handwritings have taken a whim,

> And to me, Robert Southey, petition have made,
> In a civil and nicely-penned letter—post-paid—
> That I to your album so gracious would be
> As to fill up a page there appointed for me,
> Five couplets I send you, by aid of the Nine—
> They will cost you in postage a penny a line:
> At Keswick, October the sixth, they were done,
> One thousand eight hundred and twenty and one."

Some of Southey's distractions were of his own inviting.
Soon after his arrival at Keswick, a tiny volume of poems,
entitled *Clifton Grove*, attracted his attention; its author
was an undergraduate of Cambridge. The *Monthly Review* having made the discovery that it rhymed in one
place *boy* and *sky*, dismissed the book contemptuously.
Southey could not bear to think that the hopes of a lad of
promise should be blasted, and he wrote to Henry Kirke
White, encouraging him, and offering him help towards a
future volume. The cruel dulness of the reviewer sat heavily on the poor boy's spirits, and these unexpected words
of cheer came with most grateful effect. It soon appeared,
however, that Southey's services must be slight, for his new
acquaintance was taken out of his hands by Mr. Simeon,
the nursing-father of Evangelicalism. At no time had
Southey any leanings towards the Clapham Sect; and so,
while he tried to be of use to Kirke White indirectly, their
correspondence ceased. When the lad, in every way lacking pith and substance, and ripening prematurely in a heat-
ed atmosphere, drooped and died, Southey was not willing
that he should be altogether forgotten; he wrote offering
to look over whatever papers there might be, and to give
an opinion on them. "Down came a box-full," he tells Dup-
pa, "the sight of which literally made my heart ache and
my eyes overflow, for never did I behold such proofs of hu-

man industry.   To make short, I took the matter up with
interest, collected his letters, and have, at the expense of
more time than such a poor fellow as myself can very well
afford, done what his family are very grateful for, and what
I think the world will thank me for too.   Of course I
have done it gratuitously. . . . That I should become, and
that voluntarily too, an editor of Methodistical and Calvin-
istic letters, is a thing which, when I think of, excites the
same sort of smile that the thought of my pension does."
A brief statement that his own views on religion differed
widely from those of Kirke White sufficed to save Southey's integrity.   The genius of the dead poet he overrated ;
it was an error which the world has since found time to
correct.

This was but one of a series of many instances in which
Southey, stemming the pressure of his own engagements,
asserted the right to be generous of his time and strength
and substance to those who had need of such help as a
sound heart and a strong arm can give.   William Roberts,
a Bristol bank-clerk, dying of consumption at nineteen, left
his only possession, some manuscript poems, in trust to be
published for the benefit of a sister whom he passionately
loved.   Southey was consulted, and at once bestirred himself on behalf of the projected volume.   Herbert Knowles,
an orphan lad at school in Yorkshire, had hoped to go
as a sizar to St. John's ; his relations were unable to send
him ; could he help himself by publishing a poem ? might
he dedicate it to the laureate ?   The poem came to Southey,
who found it " brimful of power and of promise ;" he represented to Herbert the folly of publishing, promised ten
pounds himself, and procured from Rogers and Earl Spen-
cer twenty more.   Herbert Knowles, in a wise and manly
letter, begged that great things might not be expected of

him; he would not be idle, his University career should be at least respectable :—" Suffice it, then, to say, *I thank you from my heart;* let time and my future conduct tell the rest." Death came to arbitrate between his hopes and fears. James Dusautoy, another schoolboy, one of ten children of a retired officer, sent specimens of his verse, asking Southey's opinion on certain poetical plans. His friends thought the law the best profession for him; how could he make literature help him forward in his profession? Southey again advised against publication, but by a well-timed effort enabled him to enter Emanuel College. Dusautoy, after a brilliant promise, took fever, died, and was buried, in acknowledgment of his character and talents, in the college cloisters. When at Harrogate in the summer of 1827, Southey received a letter, written with much modesty and good feeling, from John Jones, an old serving-man; he enclosed a poem on " The Redbreast," and would take the liberty, if permitted, to offer other manuscripts for inspection. Touches of true observation and natural feeling in the verses on the little bird with "look oblique and prying head and gentle affability" pleased Southey, and he told his humble applicant to send his manuscript book, warning him, however, not to expect that such poems would please the public—" the time for them was gone by, and whether the public had grown wiser in these matters or not, it had certainly become less tolerant and less charitable." By procuring subscribers and himself contributing an Introductory Essay on the lives and works of our Uneducated Poets, Southey secured a slender fortune for the worthy old man, who laid the table none the less punctually because he loved Shakspeare and the Psalter, or carried in his head some simple rhymes of his own. It pleased Southey to show how much intellectual pleasure and moral improvement connected with such pleasure are within reach of the humblest; thus a lesson was afforded to those who would have the March of Intellect beaten only to the tune of *Ça ira.* "Before I conclude" — so the Introduction draws to an end—" I must, in my own behalf, give notice to all whom it may concern that I, Robert Southey, Poet-laureate, being somewhat advanced in years, and having business enough of my own fully to occupy as much time as can be devoted to it, consistently with a due regard to health, do hereby decline perusing or inspecting any manuscript from any person whatsoever, and desire that no application on that score may be made to me from this time forth; this resolution, which for most just cause is taken and here notified, being, like the laws of the Medes and the Persians, not to be changed."

It was some time after this public announcement that a hand, which may have trembled while yet it was very brave and resolute, dropped into the little post-office at Haworth, in Yorkshire, a packet for Robert Southey. His bold truthfulness, his masculine self-control, his strong heart, his domestic temper sweet and venerable, his purity of manners, a certain sweet austerity, attracted to him women of fine sensibility and genius who would fain escape from their own falterings and temerities under the authority of a faithful director. Already Maria del Occidente, "the most impassioned and most imaginative of all poetesses," had poured into his ear the tale of her slighted love. Newly come from Paris, and full of enthusiasm for the Poles, she hastened to Keswick to see in person her sympathetic adviser; she proved, says Southey, a most interesting person of the mildest and gentlest manners. With him she left, on returning to America, her *Zophiel* in manuscript, the publication of which he superintended.

"*Zophiel*, Southey says, is by some Yankee woman"—
Charles Lamb breaks forth—"as if there ever had been
a woman capable of anything so great!" Now, in 1837,
a woman of finer spirit, and capable of higher things than
Zophiel, addressed a letter to Robert Southey, asking his
judgment of her powers as disclosed in the poems which
she forwarded. For some weeks Charlotte Bronte waited,
until almost all hope of a reply was lost. At length the
verdict came. Charlotte Bronte's verse was assuredly
written with her left hand; her passionate impulses, crossed and checked by fiery fiats of the will, would not mould
themselves into little stanzas; the little stanzas must be
correct, therefore they must reject such irregular heavings
and swift repressions of the heart. Southey's delay in re-
plying had been caused by absence from home. A little
personal knowledge of a poet in the decline of life might
have tempered her enthusiasm; yet he is neither a disappointed nor a discontented man; she will never hear from
him any chilling sermons on the text, All is vanity; the
faculty of verse she possesses in no inconsiderable degree;
but this, since the beginning of the century, has grown to
be no rare possession; let her beware of making literature
her profession, check day-dreams, and find her chief happiness in her womanly duties; then she may write poetry
for its own sake, not in a spirit of emulation, not through
a passion for celebrity; the less celebrity is aimed at, the
more it is likely to be deserved. "Mr. Southey's letter,"
said Charlotte Bronte, many years later, "was kind and
admirable, a little stringent, but it did me good." She
wrote again, striving to repress a palpitating joy and pride
in the submission to her director's counsel, and the sacrifice of her cherished hopes; telling him more of her daily
life, of her obedience to the day's duty, her efforts to be

sensible and sober: "I had not ventured," she says, "to hope for such a reply—so considerate in its tone, so noble in its spirit." Once more Southey wrote, hoping that she would let him see her at the Lakes: "You would then think of me afterwards with the more good-will, because you would perceive that there is neither severity nor moroseness in the state of mind to which years and observation have brought me. . . . And now, madam, God bless you. Farewell, and believe me to be your sincere friend, Robert Southey." It was during a visit to the Lakes that Charlotte Bronte told her biographer of these letters. But Southey lay at rest in Crosthwaite churchyard.

"My days among the dead are past "—Southey wrote, but it is evident that the living, and not those of his own household alone, claimed no inconsiderable portion of his time. Indeed, it would not be untrue to assert that few men have been more genuinely and consistently social, that few men ever yielded themselves more constantly to the pleasures of companionship. But the society he loved best was that of old and chosen friends, or if new friends, one at a time, and only one. Next to romping with my children, he said, I enjoy a *tête-à-tête* conversation with an *old* friend or a *new*. " With one I can talk of familiar subjects which we have discussed in former years, and with the other, if he have any brains, I open what to me is a new mine of thought." Miscellaneous company to a certain extent disordered and intoxicated him. He felt no temptation to say a great deal, but he would often say things strongly and emphatically, which were better left unsaid. " In my hearty hatred of assentation I commit faults of the opposite kind. Now I am sure to find this out myself, and to get out of humour with myself; what prudence I have is not ready on demand; and so it is that

the society of any except my friends, though it may be
sweet in the mouth, is bitter in the belly." When Coleridge, in their arguments, allowed him a word, Southey
made up in weight for what was wanting in measure; he
saw one fact quickly, and darted at it like a greyhound.
De Quincey has described his conversation as less flowing
and expansive than that of Wordsworth — more apt to
clothe itself in a keen, sparkling, aphoristic form; consequently sooner coming to an abrupt close; " the style of
his mind naturally prompts him to adopt a trenchant, pun-
gent, aculeated form of terse, glittering, stenographic sentences—sayings which have the air of laying down the law
without any *locus penitentiæ* or privilege of appeal, but are
not meant to do so." The same manner, tempered and
chastened by years, can be recognized in the picture of
Southey drawn by his friend Sir Henry Taylor :—

" The characteristics of his manner, as of his appearance,
were lightness and strength, an easy and happy composure
as the accustomed mood, and much mobility at the same
time, so that he could be readily excited into any degree of
animation in discourse, speaking, if the subject moved him
much, with extraordinary fire and force, though always in
light, laconic sentences. When so moved, the fingers of his
right hand often rested against his mouth and quivered
through nervous susceptibility. But excitable as he was in
conversation, he was never angry or irritable; nor can there
be any greater mistake concerning him than that into which
some persons have fallen when they have inferred, from the
fiery vehemence with which he could give utterance to moral
anger in verse or prose, that he was personally ill-tempered
or irascible. He was, in truth, a man whom it was hardly possible to quarrel with or offend personally, and face to
face. . . . He was averse from argumentation, and would commonly quit a subject, when it was passing into that shape,

with a quiet and good-humoured indication of the view in which he rested. He talked most, and with most interest, about books and about public affairs; less, indeed hardly at all, about the characters and qualities of men in private life. In the society of strangers or of acquaintances, he seemed to take more interest in the subjects spoken of than in the persons present, his manner being that of natural courtesy and general benevolence without distinction of individuals. Had there been some tincture of social vanity in him, perhaps he would have been brought into closer relations with those whom he met in society; but though invariably kind and careful of their feelings, he was indifferent to the manner in which they regarded him, or (as the phrase is) to his *effect* in society; and they might, perhaps, be conscious that the kindness they received was what flowed naturally and inevitably to all, that they had nothing to give in return which was of value to him, and that no individual relations were established."

How deep and rich Southey's social nature was, his published correspondence, some four or five thousand printed pages, tells sufficiently. These letters, addressed, for the most part, to good old friends, are indeed genial, liberal of sympathy, and expecting sympathy in return; pleasantly egotistic, grave, playful, wise, pathetic, with a kind of stringent pathos showing through checks imposed by the wiser and stronger will. Southey did not squander abroad the treasures of his affection. To lavish upon casual acquaintance the outward and visible signs of friendship seemed to him a profaning of the mystery of manly love. "Your feelings," he writes to Coleridge, "go naked; I cover mine with a bear-skin; I will not say that you harden yours by your mode, but I am sure that mine are the warmer for their clothing." With strangers a certain neutral courtesy served to protect his inner self like the low leaves of his own holly-tree:

> " Below, a circling fence, its leaves are seen
>   Wrinkled and keen;
>   No grazing cattle through their prickly round
>   Can reach to wound;"

but to those of whose goodness and love he was well assured, there were no protecting spines:

> " Gentle at home amid my friends I'd be,
>   Like the high leaves upon the Holly-tree."

" Old friends and old books," he says, " are the best things
that this world affords (I like old wine also), and in these
I am richer than most men (the wine excepted)." In the
group of Southey's friends, what first strikes one is, not
that they are men of genius—although the group includes
Wordsworth, and Scott, and Henry Taylor—but that they
are good men. No one believed more thoroughly than
Southey that goodness is a better thing than genius; yet
he required in his associates some high excellence, extraordinary kindness of disposition or strength of moral character, if not extraordinary intellect. To knit his friends
in a circle was his ardent desire; in the strength of his
affections time and distance made no change. An old
College friend, Lightfoot, to visit Southey, made the long-
est journey of his life; it was eight-and-twenty years
since they had met. When their hands touched, Lightfoot trembled like an aspen-leaf. " I believe," says Southey, " no men ever met more cordially after so long a separation, or enjoyed each other's society more. I shall
never forget the manner in which he first met me, nor
the tone in which he said 'that, having now seen me, he
should return home and die in peace.'" But of all
friends he was most at ease with his dear Dapple, Grosvenor Bedford, who suited for every mood of mirth and

sorrow. When Mrs. Southey had fallen into her sad decay, and the once joyous house was melancholy and silent, Southey turned for comfort to Bedford. Still, some of their Rabelaisian humour remained, and all their warmth of brotherly affection. "My father," says Cuthbert Southey, "was never tired of talking into Mr. Bedford's trumpet." And in more joyous days, what noise and nonsense did they not make! "Oh! Grosvenor," exclaims Southey, "is it not a pity that two men who love nonsense so cordially and naturally and *bonâfidically* as you and I, should be three hundred miles asunder? For my part, I insist upon it that there is no sense so good as your honest, genuine nonsense."

A goodly company of friends becomes familiar to us as we read Southey's correspondence :—Wynn, wherever he was, "always doing something else," yet able, in the midst of politics and business, to find time to serve an old schoolfellow; Rickman, full of practical suggestions, and accurate knowledge and robust benevolence; John May, unfailing in kindness and fidelity; Lamb for play and pathos, and subtle criticism glancing amid the puns; William Taylor for culture and literary theory, and paradox and polysyllables; Landor for generous admiration, and kindred enthusiasms and kindred prejudices; Elmsley, and Lightfoot, and Danvers for love and happy memories; Senhora Barker, the Bhow Begum, for frank familiarities, and warm, womanly services; Caroline Bowles for rarer sympathy and sacreder hopes and fears; Henry Taylor for spiritual sonship, as of a son who is also an equal; and Grosvenor Bedford for everything great and small, glad and sad, wise and foolish.

No literary rivalries or jealousies ever interrupted for a moment any friendship of Southey. Political and relig-

ous differences, which in strangers were causes of grave
offence, seemed to melt away when the heretic or erring
statist was a friend. But if success, fashion, flattery, tested
a man, and proved him wanting, as seemed to be the case
with Humphry Davy, his affection grew cold; and an habitual dereliction of social duty, such as that of Coleridge,
could not but transform Southey's feeling of love to one of
condemning sorrow. To his great contemporaries, Scott,
Landor, Wordsworth, his admiration was freely given.
" Scott," he writes, " is very ill. He suffers dreadfully,
but bears his sufferings with admirable equanimity. . . .
God grant that he may recover! He is a noble and gen-
erous-hearted creature, whose like we shall not look upon
again." Of Wordsworth :—"A greater poet than Wordsworth there never has been, nor ever will be." " Two or
three generations must pass before the public affect to
admire such poets as Milton and Wordsworth. Of such
men the world scarcely produces one in a millennium."
With indignation crossed by a gleam of humour, he learnt
that Ebenezer Elliott, his pupil in the art of verse, had
stepped forward as the lyrist of radicalism ; but the feeling could not be altogether anger with which he remembered that earnest face, once seen by him at a Sheffield
inn, its pale grey eyes full of fire and meaning, its expression suiting well with Elliott's frankness of manner and
simplicity of character. William Taylor was one of the
liberals of liberal Norwich, and dangled abroad whatever
happened to be the newest paradox in religion. But neither his radicalism, nor his Pyrrhonism, nor his paradoxes,
could estrange Southey. The last time the oddly-assorted
pair met was in Taylor's house ; the student of German
criticism had found some theological novelty, and wished
to draw his guest into argument ; Southey parried the

thrusts good-humouredly, and at last put an end to them
with the words, "Taylor, come and see me at Keswick.
We will ascend Skiddaw, where I shall have you nearer
heaven, and we will then discuss such questions as these."

In the year 1823 one of his oldest friends made a public attack on Southey, and that friend the gentlest and
sweetest-natured of them all.   In a *Quarterly* article
Southey had spoken of the Essays of Elia as a book which
wanted only a sounder religious feeling to be as delightful as it was original.   He had intended to alter the expression in the proof-sheet, but no proof-sheet was ever
sent.   Lamb, already pained by references to his writings
in the *Quarterly*, some of which he erroneously ascribed
to Southey, was deeply wounded.   "He might have spared
an old friend such a construction of a few careless flights
that meant no harm to religion."   A long expostulation
addressed by Elia to Robert Southey, Esq., appeared in
the *London Magazine* for October, only a portion of which
is retained in the Elia Essays under the title of "The
Tombs of the Abbey;" for though Lamb had playfully resented Coleridge's salutation, "my gentle-hearted Charles,"
his heart was indeed gentle, and could not endure the pain
of its own wrath; among the memorials of the dead in
Westminster he finds his right mind, his truer self, once
more; he forgets the grave aspect with which Southey
looked awful on his poor friend, and spends his indignation harmless as summer lightning over the heads of a
Dean and Chapter.   Southey, seeing the announcement of
a letter addressed to him by Lamb, had expected a sheaf
of friendly pleasantries; with surprise he learnt what pain
his words had caused.   He hastened to explain; had
Lamb intimated his feelings in private, he would have
tried, by a passage in the ensuing *Quarterly*, to efface the

impression unhappily created ; he ended with a declaration
of unchanged affection, and a proposal to call on Lamb.
"On my part," Southey said, "there was not even a momentary feeling of anger;" he at once understood the love,
the error, the soreness, and the repentance awaiting a being so composed of goodness as Elia. "Dear Southey"
—runs the answer of Lamb—"the kindness of your note
has melted away the mist that was upon me. I have been
fighting against a shadow. . . . I wish both magazine and
review were at the bottom of the sea. I shall be ashamed
to see you, and my sister (though innocent) will be still
more so, for this folly was done without her knowledge,
and has made her uneasy ever since. My guardian angel
was absent at the time. I will make up courage to see
you, however, any day next week. We shall hope that you
will bring Edith with you. That will be a second morti-
fication ; she will hate to see us ; but come and heap em-
bers ; we deserve it, I for what I have done, and she for
being my sister. Do come early in the day, by sunlight,
that you may see my Milton. . . . Your penitent C. Lamb."

At Bristol, in 1808, Southey met for the first time the
man of all others whom he most desired to see, the only
man living, he says, " of whose praise I was ambitious, or
whose censure would have humbled me." This was Walter Savage Landor. *Madoc*, on which Southey had built
his hope of renown as a poet, had been published, and had
been coldly received ; *Kehama*, which had been begun,
consequently now stood still. Their author could indeed,
as he told Sir George Beaumont, be contented with posthumous fame, but it was impossible to be contented with
posthumous bread and cheese. " St. Cecilia herself could
not have played the organ if there had been nobody to
blow the bellows for her." At this moment, when he

turned sadly and bravely from poetry to more profitable
work, he first looked on Landor. "I never saw any one
more unlike myself," he writes, "in every prominent part
of human character, nor any one who so cordially and in-
stinctively agreed with me on so many of the most important subjects. I have often said before we met, that I
would walk forty miles to see him, and having seen him,
I would gladly walk fourscore to see him again. He talked of *Thalaba*, and I told him of the series of mythological poems which I had planned, . . . and also told him for
what reason they had been laid aside; in plain English,
that I could not afford to write them. Landor's reply was,
'Go on with them, and I will pay for printing them, as
many as you will write, and as many copies as you
please.'" The princely offer stung Southey, as he says,
to the very core; not that he thought of accepting that
offer, but the generous words were themselves a deed,
and claimed a return. He rose earlier each morning to
carry on his *Kehama*, without abstracting time from bet-
ter-paid task-work; it advanced, and duly as each section
of this poem, and subsequently of his *Roderick*, came to
be written, it was transcribed for the friend whose sympathy and admiration were a golden reward. To be
praised by one's peers is indeed happiness. Landor, liberal of applause, was keen in suggestion and exact in censure. Both friends were men of ardent feelings, though
one had tamed himself, while the other never could be
tamed; both often gave their feelings a vehement utterance. On many matters they thought, in the main, alike—
on the grand style in human conduct, on the principles of
the poetic art, on Spanish affairs, on Catholicism. The
secret of Landor's high-poised dignity in verse had been
discovered by Southey; he, like Landor, aimed at a clas-

K   7   10

sical purity of diction; he, like Landor, loved, as a shaper
of imaginative forms, to embody in an act, or an incident,
the virtue of some eminent moment of human passion, and
to give it fixity by sculptured phrase; only the repression
of a fiery spirit is more apparent in Landor's monumental
lines than in Southey's. With certain organic resemblances,
and much community of sentiment, there were large differences between the two, so that when they were drawn together in sympathy, each felt as if he had annexed a new
province. Landor rejoiced that the first persons who shared
his turret at Llanthony were Southey and his wife; again,
in 1817, the two friends were together for three days at
Como, after Southey had endured his prime affliction—the
death of his son:—

> "Grief had swept over him; days darkened round;
> Bellagio, Valintelvi smiled in vain,
> And Monte Rosa from Helvetia far
> Advanced to meet us, wild in majesty
> Above the glittering crests of giant sons
> Station'd around . . . in vain too! all in vain."

Two years later the warm-hearted friend writes from
Pistoia, rejoicing in Southey's joy: "Thank God! Tears
came into my eyes on seeing that you were blessed with
a son." To watch the happiness of children was Landor's
highest delight; to share in such happiness was Southey's;
and Arnold and Cuthbert formed a new bond between
their fathers. In 1836, when Southey, in his sixty-third
year, guided his son through the scenes of his boyhood,
several delightful days were spent at Clifton with Landor.
I never knew a man of brighter genius or of kinder heart,
said Southey; and of Landor in earlier years:—"He does
more than any of the gods of all my mythologies, for his

very words are thunder and lightning—such is the power
and splendour with which they burst out." Landor re-
sponded with a majestic enthusiasm about his friend, who
seemed to him no less noble a man than admirable a
writer:

> "No firmer breast than thine hath Heaven
>   To poet, sage, or hero given:
> No heart more tender, none more just,
>   To that He largely placed in trust:
> Therefore shalt thou, whatever date
> Of years be thine, with soul elate
> Rise up before the Eternal throne,
> And hear, in God's own voice, 'Well done!'"

That "Well done" greeted Southey many years before
Landor's imperial head was laid low. In the last letter
from his friend received by Southey—already the darkness
was fast closing in—he writes, "If any man living is ardent for your welfare, I am; whose few and almost worthless merits your generous heart has always overvalued, and
whose infinite and great faults it has been too ready to
overlook. I will write to you often, now I learn that I
may do it inoffensively; well remembering that among
the names you have exalted is Walter Landor." Alas! to
reply was now beyond the power of Southey; still, he held
Gebir in his hands oftener than any other volume of poetry, and, while thought and feeling lived, fed upon its beauty. "It is very seldom now," Caroline Southey wrote at
a later date, "that he ever names any person: but this
morning, before he left his bed, I heard him repeating
softly to himself, *Landor, ay, Landor.*"

"If it be not now, yet it will come: the readiness is all"
—this was ever present to Southey during the happy days
of labour and rest in Greta Hall. While he was disposing

his books so as to make the comeliest show, and delight-
ing in their goodly ranks; while he looked into the radiant
faces of his children, and loved their innocent brightness,
he yet knew that the day of detachment was approaching.
There was nothing in such a thought which stirred Southey to a rebellious mood; had he not set his seal to the
bond of life? How his heart rested in his home, only his
own words can tell; even a journey to London seemed too
long:—"Oh dear; oh dear! there is such a comfort in
one's old coat and old shoes, one's own chair and own fireside, one's own writing-desk and own library—with a little girl climbing up to my neck, and saying, 'Don't go to
London, papa—you must stay with Edith;' and a little boy,
whom I have taught to speak the language of cats, dogs,
cuckoos, and jackasses, etc., before he can articulate a word
of his own;—there is such a comfort in all these things,
that *transportation* to London for four or five weeks seems
a heavier punishment than any sins of mine deserve."
Nor did his spirit of boyish merriment abate until overwhelming sorrow weighed him down:—"I am quite as noisy as I ever was," he writes to Lightfoot, "and should
take as much delight as ever in showering stones through
the hole of the staircase against your room door, and hear-
ing with what hearty good earnest 'you fool' was vocifer-
ated in indignation against me in return. Oh, dear Lightfoot, what a blessing it is to have a boy's heart! it is as
great a blessing in carrying one through this world, as
to have a child's spirit will be in fitting us for the next."
But Southey's light-heartedness was rounded by a circle
of earnest acquiescence in the law of mortal life; a clear-
obscure of faith as pure and calm and grave as the heavens
of a midsummer night. At thirty he writes:—"No man
was ever more contented with his lot than I am. for few

have ever had more enjoyments, and none had ever better
or worthier hopes. Life, therefore, is sufficiently dear to
me, and long life desirable, that I may accomplish all which
I design. But yet I could be well content that the next
century were over, and my part fairly at an end, having
been gone well through. Just as at school one wished the
school-days over, though we were happy enough there, because we expected more happiness and more liberty when
we were to be our own masters, might lie as much later in
the morning as we pleased, have no bounds and do no exercise — just so do I wish that my exercises were over."
At thirty-five :—" Almost the only wish I ever give utterance to is that the next hundred years were over. It is
not that the uses of this world seem to me weary, stale,
flat, and unprofitable — God knows far otherwise! No
man can be better contented with his lot. My paths are
paths of pleasantness. . . . Still, the instability of human
happiness is ever before my eyes; I long for the certain
and the permanent." " My notions about life are much
the same as they are about travelling—there is a good deal
of amusement on the road, but, after all, one wants to be
at rest." At forty :—" My disposition is invincibly cheerful, and this alone would make me a cheerful man if I
were not so from the tenor of my life; yet I doubt whether the strictest Carthusian has the thought of death more
habitually in his mind."

Such was Southey's constant temper: to some persons
it may seem an unfortunate one; to some it may be prac-
tically unintelligible. But those who accept of the feast
of life freely, who enter with a bounding foot its measures
of beauty and of joy—glad to feel all the while the serviceable sackcloth next the skin—will recognize in Southey
an instructed brother of the Renunciants' rule.

CHAPTER VI.

In October, 1805, Southey started with his friend Elmsley
for a short tour in Scotland. On their way northward
they stopped three days at Ashestiel. There, in a small
house, rising amid its old-fashioned garden, with pastoral
hills all around, and the Tweed winding at the meadow's
end, lived Walter Scott. It was the year in which old
Border song had waked up, with ampler echoings, in the
Lay of the Last Minstrel, and Scott was already famous.
Earlier in the year he had visited Grasmere, and had stood
upon the summit of Helvellyn, with Wordsworth and
Davy by his side. The three October days, with their
still, misty brightness, went by in full enjoyment. Southey
had brought with him a manuscript containing sundry
metrical romances of the fifteenth century, on which his
host pored, as far as courtesy and the hours allowed, with
much delight; and the guests saw Melrose, that old romance in stone so dear to Scott, went salmon-spearing on
the Tweed, dined on a hare snapped up before their eyes
by Percy and Douglas, and visited Yarrow. From Ashestiel they proceeded to Edinburgh. Southey looked coldly
on the grey metropolis; its new city seemed a kind of
Puritan Bath, which worshipped propriety instead of pleasure; but the old town, seen amid the slant light of a wild,

red sunset, impressed him much, its vast irregular outline
of roofs and chimneys rising against tumultuous clouds
like the dismantled fragments of a giant's palace.   Southey was prepared to find himself and his friends of the
Lakes persons of higher stature than the Scotch *literatuli*.
Before accepting an invitation to meet him at supper,
Jeffrey politely forwarded the proof of an unpublished review of *Madoc;* if the poet preferred that his reviewer
should not present himself, Mr. Jeffrey would deny himself the pleasure of Mr. Southey's acquaintance.   Southey
was not to be daunted, and, as he tells it himself, felt nothing but good-humour on beholding a bright-faced homun-
culus of five-foot-one, the centre of an attentive circle,
ëënunciating with North-British ëëlocution his doctrines
on taste.   The lively little gentleman, who thought to
crush *The Excursion*—he could as easily crush Skiddaw,
said Southey—received from the author of *Madoc* a courtesy *de haut en bas* intended to bring home to his consciousness the fact that he was—but five-foot-one.   The
bland lips of the gods who looked down on Auld Reekie
that evening smiled at the magnanimity alike of poet and
critic.

Two years later (1807), differences having arisen between
the proprietors and the editor of the *Edinburgh Review*,
it was in contemplation to alter the management, and Longman wrote requesting Southey to review him two or three
articles " in his best manner."   Southey did not keep
firkins of criticism of first and second brand, but he was
not unwilling to receive ten guineas a sheet instead of
seven pounds.   When, however, six months later, Scott
urged his friend to contribute, Judge Jeffrey still sat on
the bench of the *Edinburgh Review*, hanging, drawing, and
quartering luckless poets with undiminished vivacity.   It

was of no use for Scott to assure Southey that the homun-
culus, notwithstanding his flippant attacks on *Madoc* and
Thalaba, had the most sincere respect for their author and
his talents. Setting all personal feelings aside, an irrecon-
cilable difference, Southey declared, between Jeffrey and
himself upon every great principle of taste, morality, and
policy, occasioned a difficulty which could not be removed.
Within less than twelve months Scott, alienated by the
deepening Whiggery of the *Review*, and by more personal
causes, had ceased to contribute, and opposite his name in
the list of subscribers Constable had written, with indignant notes of exclamation, " *Stopt ! ! !*"   John Murray, the
young bookseller in Fleet Street, had been to Ashestiel;
in " dern privacie " a bold complot was laid; why should
the Edinburgh clique carry it before them ?   The spirit
of England was still sound, and would respond to loyalty,
patriotism, the good traditions of Church and State, the
temper of gentlemen, courage, scholarship; Gifford, of the
Anti - Jacobin, had surely a sturdier arm than Jeffrey;
George Ellis would remember his swashing-blow; there
were the Roses, and Matthias, and Heber; a rival *Review*
should see the light, and that speedily; " a good plot, good
friends, and full of expectation — an excellent plot, very
good friends."

Southey was invited to write on Spanish affairs for the
first number of the *Quarterly* (February, 1809). His political opinions had undergone a considerable alteration since
the days of Pantisocracy and *Joan of Arc*. The Reign of
Terror had not caused a violent reaction against the doctrine of a Republic, nor did he soon cease to sympathize
with France. But his hopes were dashed; it was plain
that " the millennium would not come this bout."   Man
as he is appeared more greedy, ignorant, and dangerous

than he had appeared before, though man as he may be was still a being composed of knowledge, virtue, and love. The ideal republic receded into the dimness of unborn time; no doubt — so Southey maintained to the end — a republic is the best form of government in itself, as a sun-dial is simpler and surer than a time-piece; but the sun of reason does not always shine, and therefore complicated systems of government, containing checks and counter-checks, are needful in old countries for the present; bet-ter systems are no doubt conceivable — for better men. " Mr. Southey's mind," wrote Hazlitt, " is essentially san-guine, even to overweeningness. It is prophetic of good; it cordially embraces it; it casts a longing, lingering look after it, even when it is gone for ever. He cannot bear to give up the thought of happiness, his confidence in his fellow-men, when all else despair. It is the very element ' where he must live or have no life at all.' " This is true; we sacrifice too much to prudence—Southey said, when not far from sixty—and in fear of incurring the danger or the reproach of enthusiasm, too often we stifle the ho-liest impulses of the understanding and the heart. Still, at sixty he believed in a state of society actually to be realized as superior to English society in the nineteenth century, as that itself is superior to the condition of the tattooed Britons, or of the Northern Pirates from whom we have descended. But the error of supposing such a state of society too near, of fancying that there is a short road to it, seemed to him a pernicious error, seducing the young and generous into an alliance with whatever is fla-gitious and detestable.

It was not until the Peace of Amiens (1802) that Southey was restored in feeling to his own country. From that hour the new departure in his politics may be

7*

said to date. The honour of England became as dear to him as to her most patriotic son; and in the man who had subjugated the Swiss Republic, and thrown into a dungeon the champion of Negro independence, and slaughtered his prisoners at Jaffa, he indignantly refused to recognize the representative of the generous principles of 1789. To him, as to Wordsworth, the very life of virtue in mankind seemed to dwell in the struggle against the military despotism which threatened to overwhelm the whole civilized world. Whatever went along with a spirited war-policy Southey could accept. It appeared to himself that his views and hopes had changed precisely because the heart and soul of his wishes had continued the same. To remove the obstacles which retard the improvement of mankind was the one object to which, first and last, he gave his most earnest vows. "This has been the pole-star of my course; the needle has shifted according to the movements of the state vessel wherein I am embarked, but the direction to which it points has always been the same. I did not fall into the error of those who, having been the friends of France when they imagined that the cause of liberty was implicated in her success, transferred their attachment from the Republic to the Military Tyranny in which it ended, and regarded with complacency the progress of oppression because France was the oppressor. 'They had turned their faces toward the East in the morning to worship the rising sun, and in the evening they were looking eastward, obstinately affirming that still the sun was there.' I, on the contrary, altered my position as the world went round."[1]

Wordsworth has described in memorable words the sudden exaltation of the spirit of resistance to Napoleon,

[1] The words quoted by Southey are his own, written in 1809.

its change from the temper of fortitude to enthusiasm, animated by hope, when the Spanish people rose against their oppressors. "From that moment," he says, "this corruptible put on incorruption, and this mortal put on immortality." Southey had learned to love the people of the Peninsula; he had almost naturalized himself among them by his studies of Spanish and Portuguese history and literature. Now there was in him a new birth of passion at a period of life when ordinarily the crust of custom begins to encase our free spirits. All his moral ardour flowed in the same current with his political enthusiasm; in this war there was as direct a contest between the principles of evil and good as the elder Persians or the Manicheans imagined in their fables. "Since the stirring day of the French Revolution," he writes to John May, "I have never felt half so much excitement in political events as the present state of Spain has given me." Little as he liked to leave home, if the Spaniards would bury their crown and sceptre, he would gird up his loins and assist at the ceremony, devout as ever pilgrim at Compostella. A federal republic which should unite the Peninsula, and allow the internal governments to remain distinct, was what Southey ardently desired. When news came of the Convention of Cintra (1808), the poet, ordinarily so punctual a sleeper, lay awake all night; since the execution of the Brissotines no public event distressed him so deeply. "How gravely and earnestly used Samuel Taylor Coleridge"—so writes Coleridge's daughter—"and William Wordsworth and my uncle Southey also, to discuss the affairs of the nation, as if it all came home to their business and bosoms, as if it were their private concern! Men do not canvass these matters now-a-days, I think, quite in the same tone."

That faith in the ultimate triumph of good which sustains Southey's heroine against the persecution of the Almighty Rajah, sustained Southey himself during the long struggle with Napoleon. A military despotism youthful and full of vigour, he said, must beat down corrupt establishments and worn-out governments; but how can it beat down for ever a true love of liberty and a true spirit of patriotism? When at last tidings reached Keswick that the Allies were in Paris, Southey's feelings were such as he had never experienced before. "The curtain had fallen after a tragedy of five-and-twenty years." The hopes, and the ardours, and the errors, and the struggles of his early life crowded upon his mind; all things seemed to have worked together for good. He rejoiced that the whirlwind of revolution had cleared away the pestilence of the old governments; he rejoiced that right had conquered might. He did not wish to see the bad Bourbon race restored, except to complete Bonaparte's overthrow. And he feared lest an evil peace should be made. Paris taken, a commanding intellect might have cast Europe into whatever mould it pleased. "The first business," says Southey, with remarkable prevision, "should have been to have reduced France to what she was before Louis XIV.'s time; the second, to have created a great power in the North of Germany, with Prussia at its head; the third, to have consolidated Italy into one kingdom or commonwealth."

The politicians of the *Edinburgh Review* had predicted ruin for all who dared to oppose the Corsican; they ridiculed the romantic hopes of the English nation; the fate of Spain, they declared in 1810, was decided; it would be cruel, they said, to foment petty insurrections; France had conquered Europe. It was this policy of despair which roused Scott and Southey. "We shall hoist the bloody flag," writes the latter, " down alongside that Scotch ship, and engage her yard-arm to yard-arm."   But at first Southey, by his own request, was put upon other work than that of firing off the heavy *Quarterly* guns.   Probably no man in England had read so many books of travel; these he could review better, he believed, than anything else; biography and history were also within his reach; with English poetry, from Spenser onwards, his acquaintance was wide and minute, but he took no pleasure in sitting in judgment on his contemporaries; his knowledge of the literary history of Spain and Portugal was a speciality, which, as often as the readers of the *Review* could bear with it, might be brought into use.   Two things he could promise without fail—perfect sincerity in what he might write, without the slightest pretension of knowledge which he did not possess, and a punctuality not to be exceeded by Mr. Murray's opposite neighbour, the clock of St. Dunstan's.

Southey's essays — literary, biographical, historical, and miscellaneous — would probably now exist in a collected form, and constitute a storehouse of information—information often obtained with difficulty, and always conveyed in a lucid and happy style—were it not that he chose, on the eve of the Reform Bill, to earn whatever unpopularity he could by collecting his essays on political and social subjects.   Affairs had hurried forward with eager strides; these *Quarterly* articles seemed already far behind, and might safely be left to take a quiet corner in Time's wallet among the alms for oblivion.   Yet Southey's political articles had been effective in their day, and have still a value by no means wholly antiquarian.   His home politics had been, in the main, determined by his convictions on the great European questions.   There was a party of revolution in this country eager to break with the past,

ready to venture every experiment for a future of mere
surmise. Southey believed that the moral sense of the
English people, their regard for conduct, would do much
to preserve them from lawless excess; still, the lesson read
by recent history was that order once overthrown, anarchy
follows, to be itself quelled by the lordship of the sword.
Rights, however, were pleaded—shall we refuse to any man
the rights of a man? "Therapeutics," says Southey, "were
in a miserable state as long as practitioners proceeded
upon the gratuitous theory of elementary complexions; . . .
natural philosophy was no better, being a mere farrago of
romance, founded upon idle tales or fanciful conjectures,
not upon observation and experiment. The science of
politics is just now in the same stage; it has been erect-
ed by shallow sophists upon abstract rights and imaginary
compacts, without the slightest reference to habits and
history." "Order and improvement" were the words in-
scribed on Southey's banner. Order, that England might
not fall, as France had fallen, into the hands of a military
saviour of society; order, that she might be in a condition
to wage her great feud on behalf of freedom with undivided energy. Order, therefore, first; not by repression
alone—though there were a time and a place for repression also—but order with improvement as a portion of
its very life and being. Southey was a poet and a moral-
ist, and judged of the well-being of a people by other than
material standards; the wealth of nations seemed to him
something other and higher than can be ascertained by
wages and prices, rent and revenue, exports and imports.
"True it is," he writes, "the ground is more highly cultivated, the crooked hedge-rows have been thrown down,
the fields are in better shape and of handsomer dimensions, the plough makes longer furrows, there is more corn

and fewer weeds; but look at the noblest produce of the earth—look at the children of the soil, look at the seeds which are sown here for immortality!" "The system which produces the happiest moral effects will be found the most beneficial to the interest of the individual and the general weal; upon this basis the science of political economy will rest at last, when the ponderous volumes with which it has been overlaid shall have sunk by their own weight into the dead sea of oblivion." Looking about him, he asked, What do the English people chiefly need? More wealth? It may be so; but rather wisdom to use the wealth they have. More votes? Yes, hereafter; but first the light of knowledge, that men may see how to use a vote. Even the visible beauty and grace of life seemed to Southey a precious thing, the loss of which might be set over against some gain in pounds, shillings, and pence. The bleak walls and barrack-like windows of a manufactory, the long, unlovely row of operatives' dwellings, struck a chill into his heart. He contrasts the old cottages substantially built of native stone, mellowed by time, taken by nature to herself with a mother's fondness, the rose-bushes beside the door, the little patch of flower-garden—he contrasts these with the bald deformities in which the hands of a great mill are stalled.

Before all else, national education appeared to Southey to be the need of England. He saw a great population growing up with eager appetites, and consciousness of augmented power. Whence were moral thoughtfulness and self-restraint to come? Not, surely, from the triumph of liberal opinions; not from the power to read every incentive to vice and sedition; nor from Religious Tract Societies; nor from the portentous bibliolatry of the Evangelical party. But there is an education which at

once enlightens the understanding and trains the conscience and the will. And there is that great association
for making men good—the Church of England. Connect
the two—education and the Church; the progress of enlightenment, virtue, and piety, however gradual, will be sure.
Subordinate to this primary measure of reform, national
education, many other measures were advocated by Southey. He looked forward to a time when, the great struggle
respecting property over—for this struggle he saw loom-
ing not far off—public opinion will no more tolerate the
extreme of poverty in a large class of the people than it
now tolerates slavery in Europe; when the aggregation
of land in the hands of great owners must cease, when
that community of lands, which Owen of Lanark would
too soon anticipate, might actually be realized. But these
things were, perhaps, far off. Meanwhile how to bring
nearer the golden age? Southey's son has made out a
long list of the measures urged upon the English people
in the *Quarterly Review*, or elsewhere, by his father.
Bearing in mind that the proposer of these measures resisted the Reform Bill, Free Trade, and Catholic Emancipation, any one curious in such things may determine with
what political label he should be designated:—National
education; the diffusion of cheap and good literature; a
well-organized system of colonization, and especially of female emigration;[1] a wholesome training for the children
of misery and vice in great cities; the establishment of
Protestant sisters of charity, and a better order of hospital

---

[1] " With the Cape and New Holland I would proceed thus :—' Gov-
ern yourselves, and we will protect you as long as you need protec-
tion ; when that is no longer necessary, remember that though we
be different countries, each independent, we are one people.' "—R. S.
to W. S. Landor. Letters, vol. ii. p. 263.

nurses; the establishment of savings-banks in all small towns; the abolition of flogging in the army and navy, except in extreme cases; improvements in the poor-laws; alterations in the game-laws; alterations in the criminal laws, as inflicting the punishment of death in far too many cases; execution of criminals within prison walls; alterations in the factory system for the benefit of the operative, and especially as to the employment of children; national works — reproductive if possible — to be undertaken in times of peculiar distress; the necessity of doing away with interments in crowded cities; the system of giving allotments of ground to labourers; the employment of paupers in cultivating waste lands; the commutation of tithes; and last, the need for more clergymen, more colleges, more courts of law.

"Mr. Southey," said Hazlitt, "missed his way in Utopia; he has found it at old Sarum." To one of Southey's temper old Sarum seemed good, with its ordered freedom, its serious aspiration, its habitual pieties, its reasonable service, its reverent history, its beauty of holiness, its close where priests who are husbands and fathers live out their calm, benignant lives—its amiable home for those whose toil is ended, and who now sleep well. But how Southey found his way from his early deism to Anglican orthodoxy cannot be precisely determined. Certainly not for many years could he have made that subscription to the Articles of the Church of England, which at the first barred his way to taking orders. The superstition, which seemed to be the chief spiritual food of Spain, had left Southey, for the rest of his life, a resolute opponent of Catholicism; and as he read lives of the Saints and histories of the Orders, the exclamation, "I do well to be angry," was often on his lips. For the wisdom, learning,

L   1

and devotion of the Jesuits he had, however, a just respect.
Geneva, with its grim logic and stark spirituality, suited
nerves of a different temper from his. For a time Southey thought himself half a Quaker, but he desired more
visible beauty and more historical charm than he could
find in Quakerism. Needing a comely home for his spiritual affections, he found precisely what pleased him built
in the pleasant Anglican close. With growing loyalty to
the State, his loyalty to the Church could not but keep
pace. He loved her tolerance, her culture; he fed upon
her judicious and learned writers—Taylor, with his bright
fancies like the little rings of the vine; South, hitting
out straight from the shoulder at anarchy, fanaticism, and
licentiousness, as Southey himself would have liked to
hit; Jackson, whose weight of character made his pages
precious as with golden bullion. After all, old Sarum had
some advantages over Utopia.

The English Constitution consisting of Church and
State, it seemed to Southey an absurdity in politics to
give those persons power in the State whose duty it is to
subvert the Church. Admit Catholics, he said, to every office of trust, emolument, or honour; only never admit them
into Parliament. "The arguments about equal rights are
fit only for a schoolboy's declamation; it may as well be
said that the Jew has a right to be a bishop, or the Quaker an admiral, as that the Roman Catholic has a right to
a seat in the British Legislature; his opinions disqualify
him." To call this a question of toleration was impudence; Catholics were free to practise the rites of their
religion; they had the full and free use of the press; perfect toleration was granted to the members of that church,
which, wherever dominant, tolerates no other. Catholic
Emancipation would not conciliate Ireland; the great

source of Irish misery had been, not England's power, but
her weakness, and those violences to which weakness re-
sorts in self-defence; old sores were not to be healed by
the admission of Catholic demagogues into Parliament.
The measure styled Emancipation would assuredly be followed by the downfall of the Protestant Establishment in
Ireland, and by the spread of Catholicism in English society.   To Pyrrhonists one form of faith might seem as
good or as bad as the other; but the great mass of the
English people had not advanced so far in the march of
intellect as to perceive no important difference between
Catholic and Protestant doctrine, or between Catholic and
Protestant morality.   By every possible means, better the
condition of the Irish peasantry; give them employment
in public works; facilitate, for those who desire it, the
means of emigration; extend the poor-laws to Ireland,
and lay that impost on absentees in such a proportion as
may compensate, in some degree, for their non-residence;
educate the people; execute justice and maintain peace,
and the cry of Catholic Emancipation may be safely disre-
garded.

So Southey pleaded in the *Quarterly Review*.   With
reference to Emancipation and to the Reform Bill, he and
Wordsworth—who, perhaps, had not kept themselves sufficiently in relation with living men and the public sentiment of the day—were in their solitude gifted with a measure of the prophetic spirit, which in some degree explains
their alarms.   For the prophet who knows little of expe-
diency and nothing of the manipulation of parties, nothing of the tangled skein of contending interests, sees the
future in its moral causes, and he sees it in a vision.   But
he cannot date the appearances in his vision.   Battle, and
garments rolled in blood, and trouble, and dimness of an-

guish pass before him, and he proclaims what it is given
him to see.   It matters not a little, however, in the actual
event, whether the battle be on the morrow or half a century hence; and the prophet furnishes us with no chro-
nology, or at best with some vague time and times and
half a time.   New forces have arisen before the terrors of
his prediction come to pass, and therefore, when they come
to pass, their effect is often altogether different from that
anticipated.   Wordsworth and Southey were right in de-
claring that a vast and formidable change was taking place
in the England of their day: many things which they,
amid incredulous scoffs, announced, have become actual;
others remain to be fulfilled.   But the events have taken
up their place in an order of things foreign to the concep-
tions of the prophets; the fire from heaven descends, but
meanwhile we, ingenious sons of men, have set up a light-
ning-conductor.

Southey and the *Quarterly Review* were often spoken
of as a single entity.   But the *Review*, in truth, never precisely represented his feelings and convictions.   With Gifford he had no literary sympathies.   Gifford's heart was
full of kindness, says Southey, for all living creatures except authors; *them* he regarded as Isaac Walton did the
worm.   Against the indulgence of that temper Southey
always protested; yet he was chosen to bear the reproach
of having tortured Keats, and of having anonymously glo-
rified himself at the expense of Shelley.   Gifford's omis-
sions, additions, substitutions, often caused Southey's article in the *Review* to be very unlike the article which he
had despatched to the editor in manuscript.   Probably
these changes were often made on warrantable grounds.
Southey's confidence in his own opinions, which always
seemed to him to be based upon moral principles, was

high; and he was not in the habit of diluting his ink. Phrases which sounded well in the library of Greta Hall had quite another sound in Mr. Murray's office in Fleet Street.

On arriving in London for a short visit in the autumn of 1813, Southey learnt that the Prince Regent wished to confer on him the Laureateship, vacant by the death of Pye. Without consulting the Regent, Lord Liverpool had previously directed that the office should be offered to Walter Scott. On the moment came a letter from Scott informing Southey that he had declined the appointment, not from any foolish prejudice against holding it, but because he was already provided for, and would not engross emoluments which ought to be awarded to a man of letters who had no other views in life. Southey hesitated, having ceased for several years to produce occasional verses; but his friend Croker assured him that he would not be compelled to write odes as boys write exercises at stated times on stated subjects; that it would suffice if he wrote on great public events, or did not write, as the spirit moved him; and thus his scruples were overcome. In a little, low, dark room in the purlieus of St. James'—a solitary clerk being witness—the oath was duly administered by a fat old gentleman-usher in full buckle, Robert Southey swearing to be a faithful servant to the King, to reveal all treasons which might come to his knowledge, and to obey the Lord Chamberlain in all matters of the King's service. It was Scott's belief that his generosity had provided for his poorer brother bard an income of three or four hundred pounds a year. In reality the emolument was smaller and the task-work more irksome than had been supposed. The tierce of Canary, swilled by Ben Jonson and his poetic sons, had been wickedly commuted for a small sum;

the whole net income amounted to 90*l*. But this, "the very least of Providence's mercies," as a poor clergyman said when pronouncing grace over a herring, secured an important happiness for Southey : he did not employ it, as Byron puts it, to butter his bread on both sides ; he added twelve pounds to it, and vested it forthwith in an insurance upon his own life. " I have never felt any painful anxiety about providing for my family, . . ." he writes to Scott ; " but it is with the deepest feeling of thanksgiving that I have secured this legacy for my wife and children, and it is to you that I am primarily and chiefly indebted."

Croker's assurance was too hastily given. The birthday Ode, indeed, fell into abeyance during the long malady of George III. ; but the New-Year's Ode had still to be provided. Southey was fortunate in 1814 ; events worthy of celebration had taken place ; a dithyramb, or rather an oration in lines of irregular length, was accordingly produced, and was forwarded to his musical yoke-fellow, Sir William Parsons. But the sight of Southey's page, over which the longs and shorts meandered seemingly at their own sweet will, shocked the orderly mind of the chief musician. What kind of ear could Mr. Southey have ? His predecessor, the lamented Mr. Pye, had written his Odes always in regular stanzas. What kind of action was this exhibited by the unbroken State Pegasus ? Duly as each New Year approached, Southey set himself to what he called his *ode*ous job ; it was the price he paid for the future comfort of his children. While his political assailants pictured the author of *Joan of Arc* as a court-lacquey following in the train of the fat Adonis, he, with grim cheerfulness, was earning a provision for his girls ; and had it not been a duty to kiss hands on the appointment, His

Royal Highness the Prince Regent would never have seen
his poet.   Gradually the New - Year's Ode ceased to be
looked for, and Southey was emancipated.   His verse-
making as laureate occasionally rose into something higher than journeyman work ; when public events stirred his
heart to joy, or grief, or indignation, he wrote many admirable periods of measured rhetoric.   *The Funeral Song
for the Princess Charlotte* is of a higher strain ; a knell,
heavy yet clear-toned, is tolled by its finely wrought octo-
syllabics.

A few months after the battle of Waterloo, which had
so deeply moved Southey, he started with his wife, a rare
voyager from Keswick, and his little daughter Edith May,
on a pilgrimage to the scene of victory.   The aunts remained to take care of Bertha, Kate, and Isabel, with the
nine-years-old darling of all, the only boy, Herbert.   With
Bruges, " like a city of Elizabeth's age—you expect to see
a head with a ruff looking from the window," Southey was
beyond measure delighted.   At Ghent he ransacked book-
shops, and was pleased to see in the Beguinage the realization of his own and Rickman's ideas on Sisterhoods.   On a
clear September day the travellers visited the battlefield ;
the autumnal sunshine with soft airs, and now and again a
falling leaf, while the bees were busy with the year's last
flowers, suited well with the poet's mood of thankfulness,
tempered by solemn thought.   When, early in December,
they returned with a lading of toys to their beloved lake-
country, little Edith had hardly recovered from an illness
which had attacked her at Aix.   It was seven o'clock in the
evening by the time they reached Rydal, and to press forward and arrive while the children were asleep would be to
defraud everyone of the first reward earned by so long absence.   " A return home under fortunate circumstances has

something of the character of a triumph, and requires day-
light." The glorious presence of Skiddaw, and Derwent
bright under the winter sky, asked also for a greeting at
noon rather than at night. A depth of grave and tender
thankfulness lay below Southey's joy that morning; it was
twelve years since he had pitched his tent here beside the
Greta; twelve years had made him feel the touch of time;
but what blessings they had brought! all his heart's desire
was here—books, children, leisure, and a peace that passeth understanding. The instant hour, however, was not for
meditation but for triumph :—

" O joyful hour, when to our longing home
  The long-expected wheels at length drew nigh!
 When the first sound went forth, 'they come! they come!'
  And hope's impatience quicken'd every eye!
 ' Never had man whom Heaven would heap with bliss
 More glad return, more happy hour than this.'

" Aloft on yonder bench, with arms dispread,
  My boy stood, shouting there his father's name,
 Waving his hat around his happy head;
  And there a younger group his sisters came:
 Smiling they stood with looks of pleased surprise
 While tears of joy were seen in elder eyes.

" Soon all and each came crowding round to share
  The cordial greeting, the beloved sight;
 What welcomings of hand and lip were there!
  And when those overflowings of delight
 Subsided to a sense of quiet bliss,
 Life hath no purer, deeper happiness.

" The young companion of our weary way
  Found here the end desired of all her ills;
 She who in sickness pining many a day
  Hunger'd and thirsted for her native hills.

Forgetful now of suffering past and pain,
Rejoiced to see her own dear home again.

" Recovered now the homesick mountaineer
    Sate by the playmate of her infancy,
The twin-like comrade,[1]—render'd doubly dear
    For that long absence; full of life was she
With voluble discourse and eager mien
Telling of all the wonders she had seen.

" Here silently between her parents stood
    My dark-eyed Bertha, timid as a dove;
And gently oft from time to time she woo'd
    Pressure of hand, or word, or look of love,
With impulse shy of bashful tenderness,
Soliciting again the wished caress.

" The younger twain in wonder lost were they,
    My gentle Kate and my sweet Isabel:
Long of our promised coming, day by day,
    It had been their delight to hear and tell;
And now when that long-promised hour was come,
Surprise and wakening memory held them dumb.

    *   *   *   *   *   *

" Soon they grew blithe as they were wont to be;
    Her old endearments each began to seek;
And Isabel drew near to climb my knee,
    And pat with fondling hand her father's cheek;
With voice and touch and look reviving thus
The feelings which had slept in long disuse.

" But there stood one whose heart could entertain
    And comprehend the fulness of the joy;
The father, teacher, playmate, was again
    Come to his only and his studious boy;

---

[1] Sara Coleridge.

And he beheld again that mother's eye
Which with such ceaseless care had watched his infancy.

" Bring forth the treasures now—a proud display—
     For rich as Eastern merchants we return !
Behold the black Beguine, the Sister grey,
     The Friars whose heads with sober motion turn,
The Ark well filled with all its numerous hives,
Noah, and Shem, and Ham, and Japhet, and their wives.

" The tumbler loose of limb; the wrestlers twain ;
     And many a toy beside of quaint device,
Which, when his fleecy flocks no more can gain
     Their pasture on the mountains hoar with ice,
The German shepherd carves with curious knife,
Earning in easy toil the food of frugal life.

" It was a group which Richter, had he viewed,
     Might have deemed worthy of his perfect skill;
The keen impatience of the younger brood,
     Their eager eyes and fingers never still ;
The hope, the wonder, and the restless joy
Of those glad girls and that vociferous boy.

" The aged friend[1] serene with quiet smile,
     Who in their pleasure finds her own delight ;
The mother's heart-felt happiness the while ;
     The aunt's rejoicing in the joyful sight ;
And he who in his gaiety of heart,
With glib and noisy tongue performed the showman's part "

It was manifest to a thoughtful observer, says De Quincey, that Southey's golden equanimity was bound up in a
trinity of chords, a threefold chain—in a conscience clear
of offence, in the recurring enjoyments from his honourable industry, and in the gratification of his parental affec-

---

[1] Mrs. Wilson—then aged seventy-two.

tions. In the light of Herbert's smiles his father almost lived; the very pulses of his heart played in unison with the sound of his son's laughter. "There was," De Quincey goes on, "in his manner towards this child, and towards this only, something that marked an excess of delirious doating, perfectly unlike the ordinary chastened movement of Southey's affections; and something also which indicated a vague fear about him; a premature unhappiness, as if already the inaudible tread of calamity could be divined, as if already he had lost him." As a baby, while Edith was only "like an old book, ugly and good," Herbert, in spite of his Tartar eyes, a characteristic of Southey babyhood, was already beautiful. At six he was more gentle and more loving, says Southey, than you can almost conceive. "He has just learnt his Greek alphabet, and is so desirous of learning, so attentive and so quick of apprehension, that, if it please God he should live, there is little doubt but that something will come out of him." In April, 1809, Southey writes to Landor, twenty-four hours after an attack of croup which seized his boy had been subdued: "Even now I am far, very far, from being at ease. There is a love which passeth the love of women, and which is more lightly alarmed than the lightest jealousy. Landor, I am not a Stoic at home; I feel as you do about the fall of an old tree! but, O Christ! what a pang it is to look upon the young shoot and think it will be cut down! And this is the thought which almost at all times haunts me; it comes upon me in moments when I know not whether the tears that start are of love or of bitterness."

The alarm of 1809 passed away, and Herbert grew to the age of nine, active and bright of spirit, yet too pale, and, like his father, hanging too constantly over his books;

a finely organized being, delicate in his sensibilities, and prematurely accomplished. Before the snow had melted which shone on Skiddaw that day when the children welcomed home their parents, Herbert Southey lay in his grave. His disease was an affection of the heart, and for weeks his father, palsied by apprehension, and unable to put hand to his regular work, stood by the bedside, with composed countenance, with words of hope, and agonized heart. Each day of trial made his boy more dear. With a trembling pride Southey saw the sufferer's behaviour, beautiful in this illness as in all his life; nothing could be more calm, more patient, more collected, more dutiful, more admirable. At last, worn with watching, Southey and his wife were prevailed upon to lie down. The good Mary Barker watched, and it is she who writes the following lines : — "Herbert ! — that sweetest and most perfect of all children on this earth, who died in my arms at nine years of age, whose death I announced to his father and mother in their bed, where I had prayed and persuaded them to go. When Southey could speak, his first words were, ' *The Lord hath given, and the Lord hath taken away. Blessed be the name of the Lord !*' Never can I forget that moment " (1816).

"I am perfectly resigned," Southey wrote to Bedford on the most mournful of all days, "and do not give way to grief. Thank God I can control myself for the sake of others." But next morning found him weak as a child, even weaker in body than in mind, for long anxiety had worn him to the bone, and while he tried to calm and console the rest, his limbs trembled under him. His first wild wish to fly from Keswick passed away; it was good to be there near the boy's grave. Weak as he was, he flung himself upon his work. "I employ myself incessantly, taking, however, every day as much exercise as I can bear without injurious fatigue, which is not much." "It would surprise you were you to see what I get through in a day." "For the first week I did as much every day as would at other times have seemed the full and overflowing produce of three." From his early discipline in the stoical philosophy some help now was gained; from his active and elastic mind the gain was more; but these would have been insufficient to support him without a heart-felt and ever-present faith that what he had lost was not lost for ever. A great change had indeed come upon him. He set his house in order, and made arrangements as if his own death were at hand. He resolved not to be unhappy, but the joyousness of his disposition had received its death-wound; he felt as if he had passed at once from boyhood to the decline of life. He tried dutifully to make head against his depression, but at times with poor success. "I employ myself, and have recovered strength, but in point of spirits I rather lose ground." Still, there are hidden springs of comfort. "The head and flower of my earthly happiness is cut off. But I am *not* unhappy." "When I give way to tears, which is only in darkness or solitude, they are not tears of unmingled pain." All beloved ones grew more precious; the noble fortitude of his wife made her more than ever a portion of his best self. His uncle's boy, Edward, he could not love more than he had loved him before; but, "as far as possible, he will be to me hereafter," writes Southey, "in the place of my son." And in truth the blessing of Herbert's boyhood remained with him still; a most happy, a most beautiful boyhood it had been; he was thankful for having possessed the child so long; "for worlds I would not but have been his father." "I have abundant blessings left; for each and all of these I am truly thankful; but of all the blessings which God has given me, this child, who is removed, is the one I *still* prize the most." To relieve feelings which he dared not utter with his lips, he thought of setting about a monument in verse for Herbert and himself, which might make one inseparable memory for father and son. A page or two of fragmentary thoughts in verse and prose for this poetic monument exists, but Southey could not keep his imagination enough above his heart to dare to go on with it; to do so would have dissolved his heart anew. One or two of these holy scriptures of woe, truly red drops of Southey's life-blood, will tell enough of this love passing the love of women.

"Thy life was a day; and sum it well, life is but a week of such days—with how much storm and cold and darkness! Thine was a sweet spring day—a vernal Sabbath, all sunshine, hope, and promise "

   "And that name
In sacred silence buried, which was still
At morn and eve the never-wearying theme
Of dear discourse."

   "Playful thoughts
Turned now to gall and esil."

"No more great attempts, only a few autumnal flowers like econd primroses, etc."

 "They who look for me in our Father's kingdom
Will look for him also; inseparably
Shall we be remembered."

   "Come, then,
Pain and Infirmity—appointed guests,
My heart is ready."

From the day of his son's death Southey began to step
down from the heights of life, with a steadfast foot, and
head still held erect. He recovered cheerfulness, but it
was as one who has undergone an amputation seeks the
sunshine. Herbert's grave anchored him in Keswick. An
offer of 2000*l.* a year for a daily article in the *Times* did
not tempt him to London. His home, his books, his
literary work, Skiddaw, Derwentwater, and Crosthwaite
churchyard were too dear. Three years later came the
unlooked-for birth of a second boy; and Cuthbert was
loved by his father; but the love was chastened and con-
trolled of autumnal beauty and seriousness.

When the war with France had ended, depression of
trade was acutely felt in England; party spirit ran high,
and popular passions were dangerously roused. In the
spring of 1817, the Laureate saw to his astonishment a
poem entitled *Wat Tyler*, by Robert Southey, advertised
as just published. He had written this lively dramatic
sketch in the full fervour of Republicanism twenty-three
years previously; the manuscript had passed into other
hands, and he had long ceased to think of it. The skulk-
ing rogue and the knavish publisher who now gave it to
the world had chosen their time judiciously; this rebuke
to the apostate of the *Quarterly* would be a sweet morsel
for gossip-mongers to roll under the tongue, an infallible
pill to purge melancholy with all true children of progress.
No fewer than sixty thousand copies, it is said, were sold.
Wat Tyler suited well with Southey's nonage; it has a
bright rhetorical fierceness of humanity. The speech-mak-
ing radical blacksmith, " still toiling, yet still poor," his insulted daughter, her virtuous lover, the communist priest
John Ball, whose amiable theology might be that of Mr.
Belsham in his later days, stand over against the tyrant

king, his Archiepiscopal absolver from oaths, the haughty
nobles, and the servile minions of the law.   There was
nothing in the poem that could be remembered with
shame, unless it is shameful to be generous and inexperienced at the age of twenty.   But England in 1817 seemed charged with combustibles, and even so small a spark
as this was not to be blown about without a care.   The
Prince Regent had been fired at; there were committals
for treason; there were riots in Somersetshire; the swarm
of Manchester Blanketeers announced a march to London;
the Habeas Corpus was suspended; before the year was
out, Brandreth and his fellows had been executed at Der-
by.   Southey applied to the Court of Chancery for an in-
junction to restrain the publication of his poem.   It was
refused by Lord Eldon, on the ground that the publication being one calculated to do injury to society, the author could not reclaim his property in it.   There the matter might have dropped; but it seemed good to Mr. William Smith, representing liberal Norwich, where Southey
had many friends, to take his seat in the House of Commons one evening with the *Quarterly Review* in one pocket and *Wat Tyler* in the other, and to read aloud contrasted extracts showing how the malignant renegade could
play the parts, as it suited him, of a seditious firebrand
and a servile courtier.   Wynn on the spot administered a
well-deserved rebuke; Wilberforce wrote to Southey that,
had he been present, his voice would also have been heard.
Coleridge vindicated him in the *Courier*.   Seldom, indeed,
was Southey drawn into controversy.   When pelted with
abuse, he walked on with uplifted head, and did not turn
round; it seemed to him that he was of a stature to invite bespattering.   His self-confidence was high and calm;
that he possessed no common abilities, was certain: and

the amount of toil which went into his books gave him a
continual assurance of their worth which nothing could
gainsay; he had no time for moods of dejection and self-
distrust.   But if Southey struck, he struck with force,
and tried to leave his mark on his antagonist.   To repel
this attack made in the House of Commons, was a duty.
A Letter to William Smith, Esq., M.P., was written, as
Wordsworth wished, with the strength of masculine indignation; blow after blow is planted with sure effect; no
word is wasted; there is skill in the hard hitting; and
the antagonist fairly overthrown, Southey, with one glance
of scorn, turns on his heel, and moves lightly away.   " I
wish you joy," wrote Walter Scott, " of your triumphant
answer. . . . Enough of this gentleman, who I think will
not walk out of the round again to slander the conduct of
individuals."   The concluding sentences of the Letter give
in brief Southey's fearless review of his unstained career.

" How far the writings of Mr. Southey may be found to deserve a favourable acceptance from after-ages, time will de-
cide; but a name which, whether worthily or not, has been
conspicuous in the literary history of its age, will certainly
not perish. . . . It will be related that he lived in the bosom
of his family, in absolute retirement; that in all his writings
there breathed the same abhorrence of oppression and immo-
rality, the same spirit of devotion, and the same ardent wishes
for the melioration of mankind; and that the only charge
which malice could bring against him was, that as he grew
older, his opinions altered concerning the means by which
that melioration was to be effected, and that as he learnt to
understand the institutions of his country, he learnt to appre-
ciate them rightly, to love, and to revere, and to defend them.
It will be said of him that in an age of personality he ab-
stained from satire; and that during the course of his literary life, often as he was assailed, the only occasion on which

M   8*   12

he ever condescended to reply was when a certain Mr. William Smith insulted him in Parliament with the appellation of renegade. On that occasion, it will be said, he vindicated himself, as it became him to do, and treated his calumniator with just and memorable severity. Whether it shall be added that Mr. William Smith redeemed his own character by coming forward with honest manliness, and acknowledging but is not of the slightest importance to me."

One other personal strife is worthy of notice. When visiting London in 1813, he made the acquaintance of Byron. "Is Southey magnanimous?" Byron asked Rogers, remembering how he had tried his wit in early days on *Thalaba* and *Madoc*. Rogers could answer for Southey's magnanimity, and the two poets met, Southey finding in Byron very much more to like than he had expected, and Byron being greatly struck by Southey's "epic appearance." "To have that poet's head and shoulders," he said, "I would almost have written his Sapphics." And in his diary he wrote:—"Southey's talents are of the first order. His prose is perfect. . . . He has probably written too much of poetry for the present generation; posterity will probably select; but he has passages equal to anything." At a later date Byron thought Southey's *Roderick* "the first poem of the time." But when about to publish *Don Juan*, a work "too free for these very modest days," what better mode of saucily meeting public opinion, and getting a first laugh on his side, than to dedicate such a poem to a virtuous Laureate, and show that he and his fellows, who had uttered nothing base, were yet political turncoats, not entitled by any superfine morality to assume airs of indignation against him and his reprobate hero? The dedication was shown about and laughed over, though not yet printed. Southey heard of these things, and felt released from that restraint of good feeling which made him deal tenderly in his writings with every one to whom he had once given his hand. An attack upon himself would not alone have roused Southey; no man received abuse with more self-possession. Political antagonism would still have left him able to meet a fellow-poet on the common ground of literature. When distress fastened upon Leigh Hunt, whose *Examiner* and *Liberal* had never spared the Laureate, Mr. Forster did not hesitate to apply to Southey for assistance, which was declined solely because the circular put forward Leigh Hunt's political services as those chiefly entitling him to relief. "Those who are acquainted with me," Southey wrote, "know that I am neither resentful nor intolerant;" and after expressing admiration of Leigh Hunt's powers, the letter goes on to suggest that his friends should draw up a circular in which, without compromising any of his opinions, the appeal might be made solely upon the score of literary merit, "placing him thus, as it were, within the sacred territory which ought always to be considered and respected as neutral ground." Wise and admirable words! But there was one offence which was to Southey the unforgivable sin against the holy spirit of a nation's literature. To entice poetry from the altar, and to degrade her for the pleasure of wanton imaginations, seemed to Southey, feeling as he did the sanctity of the love of husband and wife, of father and child, to be treason against humanity. Southey was, indeed, tolerant of a certain Rabelaisian freedom in playing with some of the enclosed incidents of our life. "All the greatest of poets," he says, "have had a spice of Pantagruelism in their composition, which I verily believe was essential to their greatness." But to take an extrava-

gant fling in costume of a *sans-culotte*, and to play the part
of "pander-general to the youth of Great Britain," were
different things. In his preface to *A Vision of Judgment*,
Southey deplored the recent fall in the ethical spirit of
English literature, "which for half a century had been distinguished for its moral purity," and much of the guilt he
laid on the leaders of "the Satanic School." In the long-
run the interests of art, as of all high endeavour, are invariably proved to be one with the interest of a nation's
morality. It had taken many lives of men to lift literature out of the beast. From prudential virtue and the
lighter ethics of Addison it had risen to the grave moral
dignity of Johnson, and from that to the impassioned spirituality of Wordsworth. Should all this be abandoned,
and should literature now be permitted to reel back into
the brute? We know that the title "Satanic School"
struck home, that Byron was moved, and replied with brilliant play of wit in his *Vision of Judgment*. The laugh-
ers went over to Byron's side. One who would be witty
has certain advantages, if content to disregard honesty and
good manners. To be witty was not Southey's concern.
"I saw," he said, many years after, "that Byron was a
man of quick impulses, strong passions, and great powers.
I saw him abuse these powers; and, looking at the effect
of his writings on the public mind, it was my duty to de-
nounce such of them as aimed at the injury of morals and
religion. This was all." If continental critics find in
what he set down a characteristic example of the bourgeois
morality of England, we note with interest their point of
view.[1]

[1] To certain false allegations of fact made by Byron, Southey replied in *The Courier*, and reprinted his letters in *Essays, Moral and
Political*, vol. ii. pp. 183–205.

" Bertha, Kate, and Isabel," wrote Southey on June 26, 1820, " you have been very good girls, and have written me very nice letters, with which I was much pleased. This is the last letter which I can write in return ; and as I happen to have a quiet hour to myself here at Streatham, on Monday noon, I will employ that hour in relating to you the whole history and manner of my being ell-ell-deed at Oxford by the Vice-Chancellor." Public distinctions of this kind he rated, perhaps, below their true value. To stand well with Murray and Longman was more to him than any handle to his name. A similar honour from Cambridge he declined. His gold medal from the Royal Society of Literature he changed for a silver coffee-pot for Mrs. Southey. To " be be-doctored and called everything that ends in issimus," was neither any harm nor much good ; but to take his seat between such doctors as the Duke of Wellington, and—perhaps—Sir Walter Scott was a temptation. When his old school - fellow Phillimore presented Southey, the theatre rang with applause. Yet the day was, indeed, one of the heaviest in his life. Never had he stopped for a night in Oxford since he left it in 1794, intending to bid farewell to Europe for an Utopia in some back settlement of America. Not one who really loved him — for Scott could not appear — was present. When in the morning he went to look at Balliol, no one remembered him except old Adams, who had attempted to dress his hair as a freshman, and old Mrs. Adams, the laundress, both now infirm. From the tumultuous theatre Southey strolled into Christ Church walks alone. What changes time had made ! Many of the friends with whom he had sauntered there were in their graves. So brooding, he chewed the bitter-sweet of remembrance, until at length a serious gratitude prevailed. " Little girls," the letter

ends, "you know it might be proper for me now to wear
a large wig, and to be called Doctor Southey, and to become very severe, and leave off being a comical papa.
And if you should find that ell-ell-deeing has made this
difference in me, you will not be surprised. However, I
shall not come down in my wig, neither shall I wear my
robes at home."

While in Holland, in the summer of 1826, a more conspicuous honour was unexpectedly thrust upon Southey.
The previous year he had gone abroad with Henry Taylor, and at Douay was bitten on the foot by Satan, according to his conjecture, sitting squat at his great toe;
at Leyden he was obliged to rest his inflamed foot, and
there it was his good fortune to be received into the house
of the poet Bilderdijk, a delightful old erudite and enthusiast, whose charming wife was the translator of *Roderick*.
In 1826 he visited his kind friends once more, and at
Brussels received the surprising intelligence that during
his absence he had been elected a member of Parliament.
Lord Radnor, an entire stranger, had read with admiration
Southey's confession of faith concerning Church and State,
in the last paragraph of his *Book of the Church*. By his
influence the poet had been elected for the borough of
Downton : the return, however, was null, for Southey held
a pension during pleasure ; and even if this were resigned,
where was the property qualification ? This latter objec-
tion was met by Sir Robert Inglis, who desired to know
whether Southey would sit in Parliament if an estate of
300*l.* a year were purchased for him. An estate of 300*l.*
a year would be a very agreeable thing to Robert Lack-
land ; but he had no mind to enter on a new public sphere
for which he was ill qualified by his previous life, to risk
the loss of health by midnight debates, to abandon the

education of his little boy, and to separate himself more
or less from his wife and daughters. He could not be
wrong, he believed, in the quiet confidence which assured him that he was in his proper place.

Now more than ever before, Edith Southey needed her
husband's sustaining love. On the day of his return to Keswick, while amused to find himself the object of mob popularity, he learnt that one of his daughters was ailing; the
illness, however, already seemed to have passed the worst.
This appearance of amendment quickly proved deceptive;
and, on a Sunday evening in mid July, Isabel, "the most
radiant creature that I ever beheld or shall behold," passed
away, while her father was on his knees in the room below, praying that she might be released from suffering
either by recovery or by death. All that had been gone
through ten years before, renewed itself with dread exactness. Now, as then, the first day was one of stunned in-
sensibility; now, as then, the next morning found him
weak as a child, and striving in his weakness to comfort
those who needed his support; now, as then, he turned to
Grosvenor Bedford for a heart on which he might lay
his own heart prone, letting his sorrow have its way.
"Nothing that has assailed my character, or affected my
worldly fortune, ever gave me an hour's vexation, or de-
prived me of an hour's rest. My happiness has been in
my family, and there only was I vulnerable; that family
is now divided between earth and heaven, and I must pray
to remain with those who are left, so long as I can contribute to their welfare and comfort, rather than be gathered (as otherwise I would fain be) to those who are
gone." On that day of which the word Τετέλεσται is the
record, the day on which the body of his bright Isabel
was committed to earth, Southey wrote a letter to his three

living daughters, copied with his own hand for each. It
said what he could not bear to say of consolation and
admonishment by word of mouth; it prepared them for
the inevitable partings to come; it urged on them with
measureless tenderness the duty of self-watchfulness, of
guarding against little faults, of bearing and forbearing;
it told them of his own grief to think that he should ever
by a harsh or hasty word have given their dead sister
even a momentary sorrow which might have been spared;
it ended with the blessing of their afflicted father.

Sorrows of this kind, as Southey has truly said, come
the heavier when they are repeated; under such strokes
a courageous heart may turn coward. On Mrs. Southey
a weight as of years had been laid; her spirits sank,
her firmness gave way, a breath of danger shook her.
Southey's way of bearing himself towards the dead is that
saddest way—their names were never uttered; each one
of the household had, as it were, a separate chamber in
which the images of their dead ones lay, and each went
in alone and veiled. The truth is, Southey had little native hardihood of temperament; self-control with him
was painfully acquired. In solitude and darkness his
tears flowed; when in his slumbers the images of the
dead came to him, he could not choose but weep. Therefore, all the more among those whom he wished to lead
into the cheerful ways of life, he had need to keep a guard
upon his tenderness. He feared to preserve relics, and
did not like to bear in mind birthdays, lest they should
afterwards become too dangerously charged with remembrance and grief. "Look," he writes, "at some verses in
the *Literary Souvenir*, p. 113; they are written by a dear
friend of mine on the death of—you will know who "—
for his pen would have trembled in tracing the name Isa-

bel. And yet his habitual feelings with respect to those who had departed were not bitter; the dead were absent —that was all; he thought of them and of living friends at a distance with the same complacency, the same affection, only with more tenderness of the dead.

Greta Hall, once resounding with cheerful voices, had been growing silent. Herbert was gone; Isabel was gone. In 1829 Sara Coleridge went, a bride, tearful yet glad, her mother accompanying her, to distant London. Five years later, Edith May Southey became the wife of the Rev. John Warter. Her father fell back, even more than in former years, upon the never-failing friends of his library. It was in these darkening years that he sought relief in carrying out the idea, conceived long before, of a story which should be no story, but a spacious receptacle for mingled wit and wisdom, experience and book-lore, wholesome nonsense and solemn meditation. *The Doctor*, begun in jest after merry talks with Grosvenor Bedford, grew more and more earnest as Southey proceeded. "He dreamt over it and brooded over it, laid it aside for months and years, resumed it after long intervals, and more often, latterly, in thoughtfulness than in mirth, and fancied at last that he could put into it more of his mind than could conveniently be produced in any other form." The secret of its authorship was carefully kept. Southey amused himself somewhat laboriously with ascribing it now to this hand and now to that. When the first two volumes arrived, as if from the anonymous author, Southey thrust them away with well-assumed impatience, and the disdainful words, " Some novel, I suppose." Yet several of his friends had shrewd suspicions that the manuscript lay somewhere hidden in Greta Hall, and on receiving their copies wrote to thank the veritable donor; these thanks were forwarded by Southey, not with out a smile in which something of irony mingled, to Theodore Hook, who was not pleased to enter into the jest. "I see in *The Doctor*," says its author, playing the part of an impartial critic, "a little of Rabelais, but not much; more of Tristram Shandy, somewhat of Burton, and perhaps more of Montaigne; but methinks the *quintum quid* predominates?" The *quintum quid* is that wisdom of the heart, that temper of loyal and cheerful acquiescence in the rule of life as appointed by a Divine Master, which characterizes Southey.

For the third volume of *The Doctor*, in that chapter which tells of Leonard Bacon's sorrow for his Margaret, Southey wrote as follows:

"Leonard had looked for consolation, where, when sincerely sought, it is always to be found; and he had experienced that religion effects in a true believer all that philosophy professes, and more than all that mere philosophy can perform. The wounds which stoicism would cauterize, religion heals.

There is a resignation with which, it may be feared, most of us deceive ourselves. To bear what must be borne, and submit to what cannot be resisted, is no more than what the unregenerate heart is taught by the instinct of animal nature. But to acquiesce in the afflictive dispensations of Providence —to make one's own will conform in all things to that of our Heavenly Father—to say to him in the sincerity of faith, when we drink of the bitter cup, 'Thy will be done!'—to bless the name of the Lord as much from the heart when he takes away as when he gives, and with a depth of feeling of which, perhaps, none but the afflicted heart is capable—this is the resignation which religion teaches, this is the sacrifice which it requires."

These words, written with no forefeeling, were the last put on paper before the great calamity burst upon Southey. "I have been parted from my wife," he tells Gros-

venor Bedford on October 2, 1834, "by something worse
than death.   Forty years she has been the life of my life;
and I have left her this day in a lunatic asylum."

Southey's union with his wife had been at the first one
of love, and use and wont had made her a portion of his
very being.   Their provinces in the household had soon
defined themselves.   He in the library earned their means
of support; all else might be left to her with absolute confidence in her wise contrivance and quiet energy.   Beneath
the divided work in their respective provinces their lives
ran on in deep and still accord.   Now he felt for the first
time shrunk into the limits of a solitary will.   All that
had grown out of the past was deranged by a central dis-
turbance; no branch had been lopped away, but the main
trunk was struck, and seared, and shaken to the roots.
"Mine is a strong heart," Southey writes; "I will not say
that the last week has been the most trying of my life;
but I will say that the heart which could bear it can bear
anything."   Yet, when he once more set himself to work,
a common observer, says his son, would have noticed little
change in him, though to his family the change was great
indeed.   His most wretched hour was when he woke at
dawn from broken slumbers; but a word of hope was
enough to counteract the mischief of a night's unrest.   No
means were neglected which might serve to keep him in
mental and bodily health; he walked in all weathers; he
pursued his task-work diligently, yet not over-diligently;
he collected materials for work of his choice.   When, in
the spring of 1835, it was found that the sufferer might return to wear out the body of this death in her own home,
it was marvellous, declares Cuthbert Southey, how much of
his old elasticity remained, and how, though no longer happy, he could be contented and cheerful, and take pleasure

in the pleasures of others.   He still could contribute something to his wife's comfort.   Through the weary dream
which was now her life she knew him, and took pleasure in
his coming and going.

When Herbert died, Southey had to ask a friend to
lend him money to tide over the short period of want
which followed his weeks of enforced inaction   Happily
now, for the first time in his life, his income was before-
hand with his expenses.   A bequest of some hundreds of
pounds had come in ; his *Naval Biographies* were paying
him well ; and during part of Mrs. Southey's illness he was
earning a respectable sum, intended for his son's education, by his *Life of Cowper*—a work to which a painful interest was added by the study of mental alienation forced
upon him in his own household.   So the days passed, not
altogether cheerlessly, in work if possible more arduous
than ever.   " One morning," writes his son, " shortly after
the letters had arrived, he called me into his study.   ' You
will be surprised,' he said, ' to hear that Sir Robert Peel
has recommended me to the King for the distinction of
a baronetcy, and will probably feel some disappointment
when I tell you that I shall not accept it.' "   Accompanying Sir Robert Peel's official communication came a private letter asking in the kindest manner how he could be
of use to Southey.   " Will you tell me," he said, " without reserve, whether the possession of power puts within
my reach the means of doing anything which can be serviceable or acceptable to you ; and whether you will allow
me to find some compensation for the many sacrifices
which office imposes upon me, in the opportunity of marking my gratitude, as a public man, for the eminent services
you have rendered, not only to literature, but to the higher interests of virtue and religion ?"   Southey's answer

stated simply what his circumstances were, showing how unbecoming and unwise it would be to accept the proffered honour: it told the friendly statesman of the provision made for his family—no inconsiderable one—in the event of his death; it went on to speak of his recent affliction; how this had sapped his former confidence in himself; how it had made him an old man, and forced upon him the reflection that a sudden stroke might deprive him of those faculties by which his family had hitherto been supported. "I could afford to die, but not to be disabled," he wrote in his first draft; but fearing that these words would look as if he wanted to trick out pathetically a plain statement, he removed them. Finally, if such an increase of his pension as would relieve him from anxiety on behalf of his family could form part of a plan for the encouragement of literature, it would satisfy all his desires. "Young as I then was," Cuthbert Southey writes, "I could not, without tears, hear him read with his deep and faltering voice, his wise refusal and touching expression of those feelings and fears he had never before given utterance to, to any of his own family." Two months later Sir Robert Peel signed a warrant adding 300*l.* annually to Southey's existing pension. He had resolved to recognize literary and scientific eminence as a national claim; the act was done upon public grounds, and Southey had the happiness of knowing that others beside himself would partake of the benefit.

"Our domestic prospects are darkening upon us daily," Southey wrote in July, 1835. "I know not whether the past or the present seems most like a dream to me, so great and strange is the difference. But yet a little while, and all will again be at the best." While Mrs. Southey lived, a daily demand was made upon his sympathies and

solicitude which it was his happiness to fulfil. But from
all except his wife he seemed already to be dropping away
into a state of passive abstraction. Kate and Bertha silently ministered to his wants, laid the books he wanted in
his way, replenished his ink-bottle, mended his pens, stirred the fire, and said nothing. A visit to the south-west
of England in company with his son broke the long monotony of endurance. It was a happiness to meet Landor
at Bristol, and Mrs. Bray at Tavistock, and Mrs. Bray's
friend, the humble poet, Mary Colling, whose verses he
had reviewed in the *Quarterly*. Yet to return to his sor-
rowful home was best of all; there is a leap up of the
old spirits in a letter to his daughters announcing his approach. It is almost the last gleam of brightness. In
the autumn of that year (1835) Edith Southey wasted
away, growing weaker and weaker. The strong arm on
which she had leaned for two-and-forty years, supported
her down stairs each day and bore her up again at evening. When the morning of November 16th broke, she
passed quietly " from death unto life."

From that day Southey was an altered man. His spirits fell to a still lower range. For the first time he was
conscious of the distance which years had set between him
and his children. Yet his physical strength was unbroken;
nothing but snow deterred him from his walk; he could
still circle the lake, or penetrate into Borrowdale on foot.
But Echo, whom he had summoned to rejoice, was not
roused by any call of his. Within-doors it was only by a
certain violence to himself that he could speak. In the
library he read aloud his proof-sheets alone; but for this
he might almost have forgotten the sound of his own voice.
Still, he was not wholly abandoned to grief; he looked
back and saw that life had been good; its hardest moral

discipline had served to train the heart: much still remained that was of worth—Cuthbert was quietly pursuing his
Oxford studies; Bertha was about to be united in marriage
to her cousin, Herbert Hill, son of that good uncle who
had done so much to shape Southey's career. "If not
hopeful," he writes, "I am more than contented, and disposed to welcome and entertain any good that may yet be
in store for me, without any danger of being disappointed
if there should be none." Hope of a sober kind indeed
had come to him. For twenty years he had known Caroline Bowles; they had long been in constant correspondence; their acquaintance had matured into friendship.
She was now in her fifty-second year; he in his sixty-
fifth. It seemed to Southey natural that, without making any breach with his past life, he should accept her
companionship in the nearest way possible, should give to
her all he could of what remained, and save himself from
that forlorn feeling which he feared might render old age
miserable and useless.

But already the past had subdued Southey, and if any
future lay before him it was a cloud lifeless and grey. In
the autumn of 1838 he started for a short tour on the
Continent with his old friend Senhouse, his son Cuthbert,
John Kenyon, their master of the horse, Captain Jones, the
chamberlain, and Crabb Robinson, who was intendant and
paid the bills. On the way from Boulogne they turned
aside to visit Chinon, for Southey wished to stand on the
spot where his first heroine, Joan of Arc, had recognized
the French king. At Paris he roamed along the quays
and hunted bookstalls. The change and excitement seemed to have served him; he talked freely and was cheerful.
"Still," writes his son, "I could not fail to perceive a considerable change in him from the time we had last travel,

led together—all his movements were slower, he was subject to frequent fits of absence, and there was an indeci-
sion in his manner and an unsteadiness in his step which
was wholly unusual with him." He often lost his way,
even in the hotels; then laughed at his own mistakes, and
yet was painfully conscious of his failing memory. His
journal breaks off abruptly when not more than two-thirds
of the tour had been accomplished. In February, 1839,
his brother, Dr. Southey—ever a true comrade—describes
him as working slowly and with an abstraction not usual
to him; sometimes to write even a letter seemed an effort.
In midsummer his marriage to Caroline Bowles took place,
and with her he returned to Keswick in August. On the
way home his friends in London saw that he was much altered. "The animation and peculiar clearness of his mind,"
wrote Henry Taylor, "was quite gone, except a gleam or
two now and then. . . . The appearance was that of a
placid languor, sometimes approaching to torpor, but not
otherwise than cheerful. He is thin and shrunk in person,
and that extraordinary face of his has no longer the fire
and strength it used to have, though the singular cast of
the features and the habitual expressions make it still a
most remarkable phenomenon." Still, his friends had not
ceased to hope that tranquillity would restore mental tone,
and he himself was planning the completion of great designs. "As soon as we are settled at Keswick, I shall res-
olutely begin upon the *History of Portugal*, as a duty
which I owe to my uncle's memory. Half of the labour
I consider as done. But I have long since found the advantage of doing more than one thing at a time, and the
History of the Monastic Orders is the other thing to which
I shall set to with hearty good-will. Both these are works
of great pith and moment."

Alas! the current of these enterprises was already turned awry. In August it was not without an occasional uncertainty that he sustained conversation. "He lost himself for a moment; he was conscious of it, and an expression passed over his countenance which was very touching—an expression of pain and also of resignation. . . . The charm of his manner is perhaps even enhanced at present (at least when one knows the circumstances) by the gentleness and patience which pervade it." Before long the character of his handwriting, which had been so exquisite, was changed to something like the laboured scrawl of a child; then he ceased to write. Still he could read, and, even when he could no longer take in the meaning of what was before him, his eye followed the lines of the printed page. At last even this was beyond his power. He would walk slowly round his library, pleased with the presence of his cherished possessions, taking some volume down mechanically from the shelf. In 1840 Wordsworth went over to Greta Hall. "Southey did not recognize me," he writes, "till he was told. Then his eyes flashed for a moment with their former brightness, but he sank into the state in which I had found him, patting with both hands his books affectionately like a child." In the *Life of Cowper* he had spoken of the distress of one who suffers from mental disease as being that of a dream—"a dream, indeed, from which the sufferer can neither wake nor be awakened; but it pierces no deeper, and there seems to be the same dim consciousness of its unreality." So was it now with himself. Until near the end he retained considerable bodily strength; his snow-white hair grew darker; it was the spirit which had endured shattering strokes of fate, and which had spent itself in studying to be quiet.

After a short attack of fever, the end came on the 21st

of March, 1843.   Never was that "Well done!" the guerdon of the good and faithful servant, pronounced amid a
deeper consent of those who attended and had ears to
hear.   On a dark and stormy morning Southey's body was
borne to the beautiful churchyard of Crosthwaite, towards
which he had long looked affectionately as his place of
rest.   There lay his three children and she who was the
life of his life.   Skiddaw gloomed solemnly overhead.   A
grey-haired, venerable man who had crossed the hills stood
there leaning on the arm of his son-in-law; these two,
Wordsworth and Quillinan, were the only strangers present.   As the words, "ashes to ashes," were uttered, a sudden gleam of sunshine touched the grave; the wind dropped, the rain was over, and the birds had begun their songs
of spring.   The mourners turned away thinking of a good
man's life and death with peace—

     "And calm of mind, all passion spent."

CHAPTER VII.

SOUTHEY's career of authorship falls into two chief periods
—a period during which poetry occupied the higher place
and prose the lower, and a period during which this order
was reversed. His translations of romantic fiction—*Amadis of Gaul*, *Palmerin of England*, and *The Cid*—connect
the work of the earlier with that of the latter period, and
serve to mark the progress of his mind from legend to
history, and from the fantastic to the real. The poet in
Southey died young, or, if he did not die, fell into a
numbness and old age like that of which an earlier singer
writes :—

> "Elde that in my spirit dulleth me,
> Hath of endyting all the subtilité
> Welnyghe bereft out of my remembraunce."

After thirty Southey seldom cared to utter himself in
occasional verse. The uniformity of his life, the equable
cheerfulness maintained by habits of regular work, his
calm religious faith, his amiable Stoicism, left him without
the material for lyrical poetry; and one so honest and
healthy had no care to feign experiences of the heart
which were not his. Still, he could apply himself to the
treatment of large subjects with a calm, continuous energy; but as time went on his hand grew slack, and wrought

with less ease. Scarcely had he overcome the narrative
poet's chief difficulty, that of subduing varied materials to
an unity of design, when he put aside verse, and found it
more natural to be historian than poet.

The poetry of sober feeling is rare in lyrical verse. This
may be found admirably rendered in some of Southey's
shorter pieces. Although his temper was ardent and
hopeful, his poems of pensive remembrance, of meditative
calm, are perhaps the most characteristic. Among these
his *Inscriptions* rank high. Some of those in memory of
the dead are remarkable for their fine poise of feeling, all
that is excessive and transitory having been subdued ; for
the tranquil depths of sorrow and of hope which lie beneath their clear, melodious words.

Southey's larger poetical works are fashioned of two
materials which do not always entirely harmonize. First,
material brought from his own moral nature ; his admiration of something elevated in the character of man or
woman — generosity, gentleness, loyalty, fortitude, faith.
And, secondly, material gathered from abroad ; mediæval
pomps of religion and circumstance of war ; Arabian marvels, the work of the enchanters and the genii ; the wild
beauties and adventure of life amid New-World tribes ; the
monstrous mythology of the Brahman. With such material the poet's inventive talent deals freely, rearranges de-
tails or adds to them ; still Southey is here rather a *finder*
than a *maker*. His diligence in collecting and his skill
in arranging were so great that it was well if the central
theme did not disappear among manifold accessories. One
who knows Southey, however, can recognize his ethical
spirit in every poem. Thalaba, as he himself confessed,
is a male Joan of Arc. Destiny or Providence has marked alike the hero and the heroine from mankind ; the

sheepfold of Domremi, and the palm-grove by old Moath's tent, alike nurture virgin purity and lofty aspiration. Thalaba, like Joan, goes forth a delegated servant of the Highest to war against the powers of evil; Thalaba, like Joan, is sustained under the trials of the way by the sole talisman of faith. We are not left in doubt as to where Southey found his ideal. Mr. Barbauld thought *Joan of Arc* was modelled on the Socinian Christ. He was mistaken; Southey's ideal was native to his soul. "Early admiration, almost adoration of Leonidas; early principles of Stoicism derived from the habitual study of Epictetus, and the French Revolution at its height when I was just eighteen—by these my mind was moulded." And from these, absorbed into Southey's very being, came Thalaba and Joan.

The word *high-souled* takes possession of the mind as we think of Southey's heroic personages. Poetry, he held, ought rather to elevate than to affect—a Stoical doctrine transferred to art, which meant that his own poetry was derived more from admiration of great qualities than from sympathy with individual men or women. Neither the quick and passionate tenderness of Burns nor the stringent pathos of Wordsworth can be found in Southey's verse. No eye probably ever shed a tear over the misery of Ladurlad and his persecuted daughter. She, like the lady in *Comus*, is set above our pity and perhaps our love. In *Kehama*, a work of Southey's mature years, the chivalric ardour of his earlier heroes is transformed into the sterner virtues of fortitude and an almost despairing constancy. The power of evil, as conceived by the poet, has grown more despotic; little can be achieved by the light-winged Glendoveer—a more radiant Thalaba—against the Rajah; only the lidless eye of Seeva can destroy that tyranny of

lust and pride. *Roderick* marks a higher stage in the de-
velopment of Southey's ethical ideal. Roderick, too, is a
delegated champion of right against force and fraud; he
too endures mighty pains. But he is neither such a com-
batant, pure and intrepid, as goes forth from the Arab
tent, nor such a blameless martyr as Ladurlad. He is first
a sinner enduring just punishment; then a stricken penitent; and from his shame and remorse he is at last uplifted by enthusiasm, on behalf of his God and his people, into
a warrior saint, the Gothic Maccabee.

Madoc stands somewhat away from the line of Southey's other narrative poems. Though, as Scott objected,
the personages in *Madoc* are too nearly abstract types,
Southey's ethical spirit dominates this poem less than any
of the others. The narrative flows on more simply. The
New-World portion tells a story full of picturesque incident, with the same skill and grace that belong to Southey's best prose writings. Landor highly esteemed *Madoc*.
Scott declared that he had read it three times since his
first cursory perusal, and each time with increased admiration of the poetry. Fox was in the habit of reading aloud
after supper to eleven o'clock, when it was the rule at St.
Ann's Hill to retire; but while *Madoc* was in his hand, he
read until after midnight. Those, however, who opened
the bulky quarto were few: the tale was out of relation
with the time; it interpreted no need, no aspiration, no
passion of the dawn of the present century. And the
mind of the time was not enough disengaged to concern itself deeply with the supposed adventures of a Welsh prince
of the twelfth century among the natives of America.

At heart, then, Southey's poems are in the main the
outcome of his moral nature; this we recognize through
all disguises — Mohammedan, Hindoo, or Catholic. He

planned and partly wrote a poem — *Oliver Newman* —
which should associate his characteristic ideal with Puritan
principles and ways of life. The foreign material
through which his ethical idea was set forth went far,
with each poem, to determine its reception by the public.
Coleridge has spoken of "the pastoral charm and wild,
streaming lights of the *Thalaba*." Dewy night moon-
mellowed, and the desert-circle girdled by the sky, the
mystic palace of Shedad, the vernal brook, Oneiza's favourite kidling, the lamp-light shining rosy through the
damsel's delicate fingers, the aged Arab in the tent-door—
these came with a fresh charm into English narrative poetry eighty years ago. The landscape and the manners
of Spain, as pictured in *Roderick*, are of marked grandeur
and simplicity. In *Kehama*, Southey attempted a bolder
experiment; and although the poem became popular, even
a well-disposed reader may be allowed to sympathize with
the dismay of Charles Lamb among the monstrous gods:
"I never read books of travels, at least not farther than
Paris or Rome. I can just endure Moors, because of their
connexion as foes with Christians; but Abyssinians, Ethi-
ops, Esquimaux, Dervises, and all that tribe I hate. I believe I fear them in some manner. A Mohammedan tur-
ban on the stage, though enveloping some well-known
face, . . . does not give me unalloyed pleasure. I am a
Christian, Englishman, Londoner, Templar. God help me
when I come to put off these snug relations, and to get
abroad into the world to come."

Though his materials are often exotic, in style Southey
aimed at the simplicity and strength of undefiled English.
If to these melody was added, he had attained all he desired. To conversations with William Taylor about German poetry — certainly not to Taylor's example—he as-

cribes his faith in the power of plain words to express in
poetry the highest thoughts and strongest feelings. He
perceived, in his own day, the rise of the ornate style,
which has since been perfected by Tennyson, and he regarded it as a vice in art. In early years Akenside had
been his instructor; afterwards he owed more to Landor
than to any other master of style. From *Madoc* and *Roderick*—both in blank-verse—fragments could be severed
which might pass for the work of Landor; but Southey's
free and facile manner, fostered by early reading of Ariosto, and by constant study of Spenser, soon reasserts itself; from under the fragment of monumental marble,
white almost as Landor's, a stream wells out smooth and
clear, and lapses away, never dangerously swift nor mys
teriously deep. On the whole, judged by the highest
standards, Southey's poetry takes a midmost rank; it neither renders into art a great body of thought and passion,
nor does it give faultless expression to lyrical moments.
But it is the output of a large and vigorous mind, amply
stored with knowledge; its breath of life is the moral
ardour of a nature strong and generous, and therefore it
can never cease to be of worth.

Southey is at his best in prose. And here it must be
borne in mind that, though so voluminous a writer, he did
not achieve his most important work, the *History of Portugal*, for which he had gathered vast collections. It cannot be doubted that this, if completed, would have taken a
place among our chief histories. The splendour of story
and the heroic personages would have lifted Southey into
his highest mood. We cannot speak with equal confidence of his projected work of second magnitude, the
History of the Monastic Orders. Learned and sensible it
could not fail to be, and Southey would have recognized

the more substantial services of the founders and the
brotherhoods; but he would have dealt by methods too
simple with the psychology of religious emotions; the
words enthusiasm and fraud might have risen too often to
his lips; and at the grotesque humours of the devout,
which he would have exhibited with delight, he might
have been too prone to smile.

As it is, Southey's largest works are not his most admirable. *The History of Brazil*, indeed, gives evidence of
amazing patience, industry, and skill; but its subject nec-
essarily excludes it from the first rank. At no time
from the sixteenth to the nineteenth century was Brazil a
leader or a banner-bearer among lands. The life of the
people crept on from point to point, and that is all; there
are few passages in which the chronicle can gather itself
up, and transform itself into a historic drama. Southey
has done all that was possible; his pages are rich in facts,
and are more entertaining than perhaps any other writer
could have made them. His extraordinary acquaintance
with travel gave him many advantages in narrating the
adventures of early explorers; and his studies in ecclesiastical history led him to treat with peculiar interest the
history of the Jesuit Reductions.

The History of the Peninsular War suffers by compar-
ison with the great work of Sir William Napier. That
heroic man had himself been a portion of the strife; his
senses, singularly keen, were attuned to battle; as he wrote,
the wild bugle-calls, the measured tramp, the peals of mus-
ketry, the dismal clamour, sounded in his ears; he abandoned himself again to the swiftness and "incredible
fury" of the charge. And with his falcon eye he could
discern amid the shock or formless dispersion, wherever
hidden, the fiery heart of victory. Southey wrought in

9*

his library as a man of letters; consulted sources, turned over manuscripts, corresponded with witnesses, set his material in order. The passion of justice and an enthusiasm on behalf of Spain give unity to his work. If he estimated too highly the disinterestedness and courage of the people of the Peninsula, the illusion was generous. And it may be that enduring spiritual forces become apparent to a distant observer, which are masked by accidents of the day and hour from one who is in their midst.

History as written by Southey is narrative rendered spiritual by moral ardour. There are no new political truths, he said. If there be laws of a nation's life other than those connected with elementary principles of morality, Southey did not discover these. What he has written may go only a little way towards attaining the ultimate ends of historical study, but so far as it goes it keeps the direct line. It is not led astray by will-o'-the-wisp, vague-shining theories that beguile night wanderers. Its method is an honest method as wholesome as sweet; and simple narrative, if ripe and sound at first, is none the less so at the end of a century.

In biography, at least, one may be well pleased with clear and charming narrative. Here Southey has not been surpassed, and even in this single province he is versatile; he has written the life of a warrior, of a poet, and of a saint. His industry was that of a German; his lucidity and perfect exposition were such as we rarely find outside a French memoir. There is no style fitter for continuous narrative than the pedestrian style of Southey. It does not beat upon the ear with hard, metallic vibration. The sentences are not cast by the thousand in one mould of cheap rhetoric, nor made brilliant with one cheap colour. Never dithyrambic, he is never dull; he affects neither the trick of stateliness nor that of careless ease; he does not seek out curiosities of refinement, nor caress delicate affectations. Because his style is natural, it is inimitable, and the only way to write like Southey is to write well.

"The favourite of my library, among many favourites;" so Coleridge speaks of the *Life of Wesley*—"the book I can read for the twentieth time, when I can read nothing else at all." And yet the schoolboy's favourite—the *Life of Nelson*—is of happier inspiration. The simple and chivalric hero, his splendid achievements, his pride in duty, his patriotism, roused in Southey all that was most strong and high; but his enthusiasm does not escape in lyrical speech. "The best eulogy of Nelson," he says, "is the faithful history of his actions; the best history that which shall relate them most perspicuously." Only when all is over, and the captain of Trafalgar lies dead, his passion and pride find utterance :—"If the chariot and the horses of fire had been vouchsafed for Nelson's translation, he could scarcely have departed in a brighter blaze of glory." From Nelson on the quarter-deck of the *Victory*, to Cowper caressing his tame hares, the interval is wide; but Southey, the man of letters, lover of the fireside, and patron of cats, found it natural to sympathize with his brother poet. His sketches of literary history in the *Life of Cowper* are characteristic. The writer's range is wide, his judgment sound, his enjoyment of almost everything literary is lively; as critic he is kindly yet equitable. But the highest criticism is not his. Southey's vision was not sufficiently penetrative; he culls beauties, but he cannot pluck out the heart of a mystery.

His translations of romantic fiction, while faithful to their sources, aim less at literal exactitude than at giving the English reader the same pleasure which the Spaniard

receives from the originals.   From the destruction of Don
Quixote's library Master Nicholas and the curate spared
Amadis of Gaul and *Palmerin of England.*   Second to
Malory's grouping of the Arthur cycle *Amadis* may well
take its place.   Its chivalric spirit, its wildness, its tenderness and beauty, are carefully preserved by the translator.
But Southey's chief gift in this kind to English readers is
The Cid.   The poem he supposed, indeed, to be a metrical
chronicle instead of a metrical romance—no fatal error;
weaving together the best of the poem, the ballads and the
chronicle, he produced more than a mere compilation.   " I
know no work of the kind in our language," wrote Coleridge, " none which, uniting the charms of romance and
history, keeps the imagination so constantly on the wing,
and yet leaves so much for after-reflection."

Of Southey's political writings something has been said
in a former chapter.   Among works which can be brought
under no general head, one that pleased the public was
Espriella's Letters, sketches of English landscape, life, and
manners, by a supposed Spanish traveller.   The letters, giving as they do a lively view of England at the beginning
of the present century, still possess an interest.   Apart
from Southey's other works stands *The Doctor ;* nowhere
else can one find so much of his varied erudition, his genial spirits, his meditative wisdom.   It asks for a leisurely
reader content to ramble everywhere and no whither, and
still pleased to take another turn because his companion
has not yet come to an end of learning, mirth, or meditation.   That the author of a book so characteristic was not
instantly recognized, is strange.   " The wit and humour
of *The Doctor,*" says Edgar Poe, a keen critic, " have seldom been equalled.   We cannot think Southey wrote
it."   Gratitude is due to Dr. Daniel Dove from innumer-

able "good little women and men," who have been delighted with his story of *The Three Bears*.   To know that he had added a classic to the nursery would have been the pride of Southey's heart.   Wide eyes entranced and peals of young laughter still make a triumph for one whose spirit, grave with a man's wisdom, was pure as the spirit of a little child.

THE END.